NOT ASHAMED
—— OF THE ——
GOSPEL

*New Testament Interpretations
of the Death of Christ*

The Didsbury Lectures

The Didsbury Lectures are delivered annually at the
Nazarene Theological College, Manchester

The following series are available:

F. F. BRUCE, *Men and Movements in the Primitive
Church*
I. H. MARSHALL, *Last Supper and Lord's Supper*
T. F. TORRANCE, *The Mediation of Christ*
J. ATKINSON, *Martin Luther: Prophet to the Church
Catholic*
C. K. BARRETT, *Church, Ministry & Sacraments in the
New Testament*
D. GUTHRIE, *The Relevance of John's Apocalypse*
R. E. CLEMENTS, *Wisdom in Theology*
C. E. GUNTON, *Christ and Creation*
J. D. G. DUNN, *Christian Liberty*

NOT ASHAMED
—— OF THE ——
GOSPEL

*New Testament Interpretations
of the Death of Christ*

Morna D. Hooker

THE PATERNOSTER PRESS
Carlisle UK

British Library Cataloguing in Publication Data

Hooker, Morna D.
  Not Ashamed of the Gospel : New Testament
  Interpretations of the Death of Christ
  I. Title
  226.06

  ISBN 0–85364–543–4

Typeset by Photoprint, Torquay, Devon
and printed in the UK for The Paternoster Press,
PO Box 300, Carlisle, Cumbria, CA3 0QS
by The Guernsey Press Co. Ltd., Guernsey, Channel Islands

Contents

Preface

These studies are based on the Didsbury Lectures, delivered at the British Isles Nazarene College, Didsbury, Manchester, in October 1988, and on the Brennan Lectures, given in St. Matthew's Episcopal Church, Louisville, at the invitation of the Diocese of Kentucky, in January 1989. I am grateful for the warm welcome and generous hospitality shown to me (and in Kentucky to my husband also) by both communities.

In the original four lectures I was able to consider the approach of only three of our New Testament writers to the problem of the death of Christ. In the interests of presenting a more balanced and complete picture, it seemed necessary to look – however briefly – at the whole scene. Chapters 4–5, 7–8 have therefore been added. The remaining chapters incorporate the original lectures, though often with extensive additions. Since Paul's theology is notoriously difficult, some readers may prefer to read chapters 3–6 **before** chapter 2.

I must apologize to those who asked to read these lectures when they were delivered for the long delay in publishing them. Other commitments prevented me from doing the necessary work of revision and expansion until now. I hope the result will be useful to those who are eager to learn – as were the audiences at the lectures – from those who in the early days of the Christian Church attempted in various ways to express the inexpressible grace which they had experienced through the death and resurrection of Christ.

I am grateful to Arnold Browne and John Sweet for their comments on the chapter on Hebrews and the section on Revelation respectively, and to Anthony and Melanie Bash for their help in reading the proofs. Above all I am grateful to my husband, David Stacey, who died just as the manuscript was completed, for his encouragement and advice at every stage. Needless to say, the responsibility for any errors remains mine.

M. D. H.
Cambridge

CHAPTER ONE

Introduction

There is no doubt that the death of Jesus lies at the heart of the Christian gospel, and therefore of the New Testament. There could be no topic more important for us to consider, and nothing richer in its meaning. It is a vast subject, and even if we confine ourselves to New Testament teaching, we can only begin to explore its significance. We shall not be concerned in this book with the historical problems of the date of the crucifixion or the nature of the trials[1] – not because history is unimportant, but because there is not sufficient space to treat everything, and because history without interpretation is nothing. The fact that Jesus has died can hardly be described as good news; the belief that he died for our sins is – but what a complexity of ideas is hidden in the statement that 'he died for our sins'! The problem lies in that tiny word 'for'. The statement that 'he died' is clear enough; as for the notion of 'our sins', we find that all too comprehensible. But how are his death and our sins related? What does that tiny word 'for' signify? It has often been said that there is no one orthodox doctrine of the atonement; the Church has never been able to sum up the meaning of the death of Christ in a credal statement because the experiences which men and women have of the reconciling love of God are many and various. Something of this variety is already opening up in the pages of the New Testament, as men grappled with the stupendous question: Why did Christ die? What I hope to do in this book is to explore a few of the many different ways in which the death of Jesus came to be explained and interpreted by our New Testament authors.

---

1 We must leave aside the question of Jesus' own understanding of his approaching death: that he foresaw its likelihood and accepted his fate as God's will seems clear, but the exact manner in which he interpreted it is a much more complex problem. We are concerned here with the various ways in which his *followers* understood it.

Our first problem, in looking at the New Testament understanding of the death of Jesus, is that of putting ourselves back into the situation of first-generation Christians. We need not only to forget the discussions about the atonement which took place in the later Church, but to transfer ourselves from a culture in which the cross is an honoured symbol to one in which it signified utter degradation. Our problem is simply that we are too used to the Christian story; it is difficult for us to grasp the absurdity – indeed, the sheer madness – of the gospel about a crucified saviour which was proclaimed by the first Christians in a world where the cross was the most barbaric form of punishment which men could devise.[2]

Crucifixion was a common form of execution in the ancient world. If references to it in ancient literature are comparatively rare, this is because the topic was unpleasant – hardly the sort of thing on which ladies and gentlemen cared to dwell. In a speech defending a Roman who had been threatened with the death penalty, Cicero protested that the very word 'cross' should be far removed from the thoughts, eyes and ears of a Roman citizen.[3] We may well share this reluctance to dwell on its horrors, but if we are to understand the significance of the gospel as it was proclaimed in the first century it is essential that we grasp just what crucifixion entailed. And though a Roman citizen might go through life without a thought for those who suffered this barbaric penalty, things were very different if one belonged to the have-nots of society; if one were a slave, or a traitor, or an opponent of Rome, then it was impossible not to think about what it entailed, for the chances of ending up on a cross were all too high. The frequency with which crucifixion was used as a mode of punishment was partly due to the fact that the victim died a lingering and horribly painful death; one could therefore inflict the maximum pain on one's enemies or on the criminals being punished; and partly it was due to the fact that nailing a man up naked – whether dead or alive – was the greatest possible indignity to which one could subject him. Crucifixion thus combined the death penalty with excruciating torture and with total humiliation; hanging, by comparison, was a merciful death. Even the flogging which often preceded crucifixion could

---

2 In much of what follows I am indebted to the admirable survey by Martin Hengel, *Crucifixion*, London 1977.
3 *Pro Rabirio* 16.

prove a mitigation of the punishment, in that it sapped the victim's strength and shortened the time of torture, which could sometimes last for days.

Crucifixion was thus an utterly gruesome business – a cruel and sadistic form of execution: it is hardly surprising that the Jewish historian Josephus described it as 'the most wretched of deaths'.[4] In the Roman Empire it was used primarily to punish slaves: the threat of crucifixion was used to keep slaves subservient, and the threat was no idle one, for the punishment was often carried out. But it was used also to punish traitors (even Roman citizens, who by their treachery lost their rights) and of course rebellious subject people such as the Jews.

No wonder, then, that Paul recognized that his proclamation of Christ on the cross was sheer folly. The idea of a dying God was not without precedent in the ancient world, but a gospel about a *crucified* Lord was something quite different! Here, incidentally, is the real answer to those who from time to time have attempted to argue that Jesus never existed: men might have made up a story about a preacher and a healer, but never would they have invented such a crazy gospel as this. The cross was a symbol of weakness – of total impotence. The dying Jesus was taunted because he could not save himself – and neither, so it seemed, could his God. The cross also signified total humiliation and degradation. In proclaiming a crucified Messiah as 'good news', the first Christians clearly faced problems. People just did not wish to think about crucifixion, whether they were among the better-off members of society, or whether they belonged to the lower orders, for whom the possibility of crucifixion was all too real a possibility. This is the scandal of the message of the cross. Imagine how Jesus' call to take up one's cross and follow him to the gallows would sound to men and women in this context! It is hardly the kind of call to win converts; for first-century slaves, good news would be how to *escape* such punishment, not a summons to embrace it.

The scandal of the cross was thus not simply that Jesus had been put to death as a criminal, but that the particular death he had suffered was the most barbaric that could be devised. Moreover, this barbaric death had involved the display of his naked body in public – the final, utter degradation. Christian artists, not unnaturally, have shied

---

4 *De Bello Judaico* 7.203.

away from this aspect of Christ's suffering: they have had no inhibitions about portraying the blood, caused by the crown of thorns and the spear-thrust, for these proclaim the truth that Christ's blood was shed for us; but they have shrunk from portraying the nakedness of Christ – the modest loincloth which they add to his body conceals the shame that was an integral part of crucifixion. But the early Christians were very much aware of this as an essential part of the scandal of the cross. One second-century writer, Melito, Bishop of Sardis, wrote a Homily on the Passion which includes these lines:

'He who hung the earth is hanging;
he who fixed the heavens has been fixed;
he who fastened the universe has been fastened to a tree . . .
O unprecedented murder! Unprecedented crime!
The Sovereign has been made unrecognizable by his naked body,
and is not even allowed a garment to keep him from view.
That is why the lights of heaven turned away,
and the day was darkened.'[5]

Crucifixion was widely practised by the Roman authorities, for it was the kind of punishment which appealed to those whose concern was to preserve law and order. It was not, however, used by Jews. The normal form of execution laid down in the Jewish law was by stoning. The criminal who offended against the law had to be destroyed. Because he was an outcast from society, he came under the curse of God, and the power of the divine curse was such that the criminal in turn became a source of contamination – that is, he became the curse of God – to others. So we read in Deut. 21.23 that the criminal who is put to death and hung on a tree must not remain on the tree overnight, because he is cursed by God and his body would defile the land; therefore he must be buried before nightfall. What we have here is not a reference to crucifixion or to hanging, but to the display of a criminal's corpse on a tree after he has been put to death by stoning. His body is displayed there as a sign of his humiliation and rejection; he no longer belongs to the people of God, and is thus an outcast. But it is easy to see how the words of Deut. 21.23 could be applied at a later time to those who were crucified; for victims of crucifixion were also hung up on a tree – and this was taken as a clear sign that they had fallen under the curse of God.

---

5 Melito, *Homily on the Passion*, 96f. Translation based on that by S. G. Hall, *Melito of Sardis* (Oxford Early Christian Texts), Oxford 1979.

Throughout their occupation of Palestine the Romans used crucifixion in subjugating the Jews. Thousands of Jewish rebels were crucified, yet those who suffered this form of death were never identified as Jewish martyrs. This is hardly surprising, since those whose bodies were exposed on a tree were an offence to God, as Deut. 21.23 says, and the very form of their death was a demonstration that they were *not* innocent in his sight. One recent writer has queried this interpretation, arguing that these men died as Jewish patriots and would therefore have been regarded as martyrs[6] – but for this we have no evidence. This blank silence suggests that their form of death was an embarrassment. Those who were executed in other ways could be seen as martyrs, as righteous sufferers, but those who suffered this particular humiliation were assumed to have come under the curse of God – a clear indication that they had offended him. It can be argued, of course, that this was a Roman punishment, and had nothing to do with God's verdict upon them, and that there was therefore no reason to suppose that the curse of Deut. 21.23 was relevant.[7] Even if we allow this, it makes no difference in the case of Jesus. For the Gospels insist that though he was put to death by the Romans, it was the Jews who brought accusations against him of law-breaking, of attacking the temple, and of blasphemy. They stress that the judgement that Jesus was worthy of death was pronounced in a Jewish court by a Jewish judge:[8] the verdict of Deut. 21.23 would certainly be thought to apply to him.

It is no wonder, then, that Paul, in writing to the Corinthians, described his message of 'Christ crucified', not simply as 'foolishness' – for so it must have seemed to men and women of every race and social class – but as a 'stumbling-block' to the Jews in particular. The problem was not caused by the fact that Christ had endured suffering, for though the Deuteronomic law had apparently promised prosperity and long life to the righteous, the Jews had long since had to grapple with the fact that this is not a fair world, and that it is simply not true that the righteous are always rewarded and the wicked punished. They had come

6 Paula Fredriksen, 'Paul and Augustine: Conversion Narratives, Orthodox Traditions, and the Retrospective Self', *J.T.S.* n.s. 37, 1986, pp. 12f.
7 Ibid, pp. 10–13.
8 Some scholars minimize the role of the Jews in the death of Jesus; see, e.g., P. Winter, *On The Trial of Jesus*, Berlin 1961. Nevertheless, it seems well-nigh certain that they were involved to some extent; cf. D. R. Catchpole's response to Winter in *The Trial of Jesus*, Leiden 1971.

to recognize that the righteous are often synonymous with the 'poor', and that the wicked often enjoy prosperity; it was possible, then, that God's Messiah might himself be identified with the righteous poor, and share their suffering. Nor was the problem simply due to the fact that Christ had died, for Judaism had already had to cope with the death of martyrs for the faith. In the time of the Maccabaean uprising, men and women had been cruelly tortured and executed because of their loyalty to the Jewish law, but by now the hope of resurrection offered a solution to their suffering and deaths: they died as martyrs, and would be rewarded hereafter by God. Thus Jesus' death was not in itself a stumbling-block for the Jews, since it was possible that God's Messiah might also suffer martyrdom – but the form of his death was another matter, for he had not died because of his loyalty to the Jewish law; on the contrary, the tradition was that he had been arraigned before the Jewish court as a blasphemer and a law-breaker, and the judgement of that court was apparently confirmed by the fact that he had been crucified, his body exposed naked on a tree. Here was the proof that the Sanhedrin's verdict was correct: the form of Jesus' death was a clear indication that he was under the curse of God, a lawbreaker and blasphemer, and that he had been excommunicated from God's people, cut off from them because of his own wickedness. Here is a 'stumbling-block', a scandal indeed! It was a scandal of such proportions that it led in turn to another problem – the failure of Israel to respond to the Gospel. How was this to be explained? If Jesus was God's Messiah, or anointed one, and if his death and resurrection were part of the divine plan, why did his people fail to accept him? Had God's purposes failed?

The first task of the early Christian preachers, therefore, as they proclaimed the Gospel to their fellow-Jews, was to deal with the problem of Christ's death – to explain how someone executed as a criminal had been vindicated by God, how someone who was (according to the evidence of scripture) under the curse of God could in fact be a source of blessing to others, how someone branded as an outcast could be a saviour. The absurdity of their message is itself confirmation of the depth of the experience which led them to seek for explanations. Only the conviction that Christ had in fact been raised from the dead could have led them to proclaim this ridiculous gospel. Once again, we are too used to the Christian gospel to realize its sheer folly: we need what F. W. Dillistone described as 'a temporary suspension of belief in the Resurrection in order that the full impact of the Passion and Crucifixion of Jesus may be experienced'.[9] We need to try to place ourselves on the other side of the resurrection, if we are to grasp the scandal of the cross.

How, then, did they deal with this problem? The first, obvious, step, was to turn to the scriptures. Since scripture apparently pronounced Christ to have been under a curse, did it have some alternative explanation to offer? It was not difficult to discover scriptures which spoke of the suffering of the righteous; the psalms, in particular, described those who were faithful to God in spite of all calamities, and of their trust in him that he, in turn, would be faithful to them and deliver them, even from the jaws of death. Christ's suffering and death were in accordance with a pattern which runs through the Old Testament – a pattern of faithful allegiance to God in the face of suffering, and of subsequent vindication. There was no problem in affirming that Christ died 'in accordance with the scriptures'; that the Son of man had been delivered up into the hands of sinners, 'as it was written'. But how were they to deal with the scandal of the cross? The problem here was immense, but the logic was very simple. Everything began from their conviction of the resurrection: since Christ had been raised from the dead, this meant that he had been vindicated by God, proclaimed as Lord and Christ, and was now seated at God's right hand. But this must mean that the Romans had been mistaken in crucifying him as a criminal, and that the Jews had been wrong to condemn him as a blasphemer and a law-breaker. If death had been overcome and Christ was alive, the curse had also been annulled and changed to blessing. The scandal of the gospel of a crucified Messiah was in fact no scandal but gospel – good news for the world.

But logic never converted anyone. Only the experience of the living Lord could persuade a Jew that the verdict pronounced by the law itself on Jesus had been overthrown, that a crucified Messiah was *not* an offence to God, but a source of blessing to the nations. Christian understanding of the death of Jesus began from the experience of the resurrection, but even so, there were different ways of handling the cross itself. One obvious reaction to the Christian gospel was to revel in the good news, to exult in the experience of the living Lord, to enjoy the new life of the

9 In *The Christian Understanding of Atonement*, London 1964, p. 155.

Spirit inaugurated by the resurrection, and to forget that the decisive event which had brought it all about was the obedient death of Christ, without which there would have been no resurrection. That some Christian communities did react in this way we know from 1 Corinthians, where Paul reminds the Christian community in Corinth that the gospel he proclaimed to them is about a *crucified* Messiah (1 Cor. 1.17–2.2). When Paul states the obvious, it is usually with good cause, and when he reminds his readers of what they ought to know, it is because he feels that they have forgotten something vital. In 1 Corinthians it is clear why Paul needs to stress that the gospel is about the cross of Christ; the message is 'folly to Gentiles, a scandal to Jews'. We have already seen why the gospel would seem absurd to the whole world, and why it should be a scandal to Jews. If Paul reminds his readers of the folly and the scandal, it must be because they have deliberately 'forgotten' it, because they have shied away from the foolishness of the gospel and its scandal and have concentrated instead on the joys and benefits which follow from the resurrection. The Corinthians are so full of the joys of the Spirit that they have forgotten the significance of the symbol which lies at the heart of their faith.

Why was Paul so anxious that the Corinthians should get things in perspective? It was not simply a question of correct doctrine, for what the Corinthians were in danger of forgetting was the implication of the manner of Christ's death for their own way of life. Experience of the resurrection had led them to suppose that Christian life was totally positive – a matter of joy and excitement. Their experience had led them to interpret the Christian life in terms of instant blessing – instant joy, instant peace, instant salvation. They would certainly have felt at home in the modern world, where credit cards have – if the advertisements are to be believed – given us instant access to every comfort we can imagine, without the inconvenience of having to pay anything for it. Paul, I suspect, would have disapproved totally of credit cards: certainly he disapproves of the Corinthians' understanding of the Christian life in terms of instant enjoyment of eschatological bliss. 'What!' he writes. 'You are already full! You are already rich! You are already reigning – without us!' Note that final 'without us'. 'Would that you *were* reigning,' he continues, 'so that we might share your reign!' (1 Cor. 4.8). In Paul's view, the Corinthians are not really full at all, they are not rich, and they do not reign; they are living on false credit. The reason is that they have not faced up to the reality of the death of Christ and its significance for their life-style. In Paul's view, Christians cannot truly experience the resurrection-life of Christ unless they share also in his crucifixion – and that means accepting the shame and the scandal of the cross. So he goes on to spell out what this means for himself: 'God has exhibited us apostles like those condemned to death in the arena – a spectacle to everyone; we are foolish, weak, disgraced; we are hungry, thirsty, clothed in rags, roughly-handled, homeless, hard-working; we are reviled, persecuted, slandered, treated like the scum of the earth' (1 Cor. 4.9–13). Paul identifies himself with the scandal of the cross: there is no question of Christ's death being a substitute for his own.

But though the Corinthians played down the shame and scandal of the cross, they did not go so far as to deny that Christ had died. That suggestion came later with the emergence of docetic teaching, which held that Jesus had escaped crucifixion by changing places with Judas or with Simon of Cyrene. Such beliefs were obviously attempts to deal with the scandal at the heart of Christianity by denying it.

Why did Christ die? There are various ways of answering this question. At one level, it can be answered in terms of human reaction to Jesus. He died because Judas betrayed him, because the Jews plotted against him, because Caiaphas wanted him out of the way, because the Romans were anxious to get rid of someone who might prove to be a political agitator. He died because of human sin – because of the inability of men and women to recognize goodness when they saw it, because of their rejection of his proclamation of the Kingdom of God, because of their own mistaken notions about the demands of God. This is an answer which we find stressed in the gospels, which emphasize the responsibility of Jesus' contemporaries for his death. But at a deeper level, we can give an answer which seems to be in direct contradiction to it: Jesus died because it was the will of God that he should die. This explanation is stressed in the passion predictions: it is necessary for Jesus to die – in other words, it is part of God's plan; it is written of the Son of man that he will suffer and die – that is, it is set out in scripture as his fate. Paradoxically, the purpose of God and the rebellion of men work to the same end, since both lead to the cross. The evangelists apparently see no conflict here: in the mysterious

purpose of God, he can use even human sin to achieve his
end. We may compare what Paul says about Pharaoh in
Romans 9 – God sets him over Egypt and hardens his heart,
in order to demonstrate his own power in delivering his
people in the Exodus. So Judas, Caiaphas, Pilate, the Jewish
religious authorities and the Roman military forces, are all
pawns in the hands of God. But this does not remove their
responsibility for their actions. The evangelists play on the
double meaning of the Greek word *paradidōmi* – to hand
over. The Son of man is handed over into the hands of men:
sometimes it is Judas who hands him over – who betrays
him; sometimes it is God who hands him over – who
delivers him up into the hands of men; sometimes we
wonder whether it is the divine hander-over or the human
betrayer who is being referred to. There is no conflict, since
God is in control, even when the enemies of Jesus seem to
have triumphed: it is his purpose which is being worked out,
even when everything seems lost.

But these answers do not go far enough to satisfy us. To
say 'Jesus died because of men's wickedness' may offer an
explanation as to *how* it happened, but simply underlines
the tragedy; to say that it was the will of God that Jesus
should die may explain *why* the tragedy was allowed to
occur, but gives us no hint as to why God moves in such
mysterious ways. When we ask 'Why did Christ die?' we are
expecting to find some kind of meaning in his death.

We seek for meaning in any kind of tragedy. When a
mother asks the anguished question, 'Why did my child die?'
it is little use telling her that it was because he darted into
the road without looking, or because a drunken driver was
not in control of his vehicle. It is worse than useless to
suggest that the child's death can be attributed to the will of
God. She is looking for meaning in what appears to be a
meaningless event, searching for comfort which will help her
to come to terms with the tragedy, and it will not help her to
blame the child, or the driver, or even God. She is more
likely to find comfort by campaigning for safer roads, for
pedestrian crossings and lower speed limits – anything
which will prevent other children being killed in the same
way. We come to terms with tragedy by trying to make
positive use of it; we find meaning in death by using it as a
way of helping others to live.

Now in a sense we are still not answering the basic
question as to why the child died, for what we are dealing
with is an interpretation given to the event after it occurred

– not the reason which brought about the child's death. The child did not die in order that a campaign might be launched for safer roads; we are talking, not about the purpose of the child's accident, but about the good that has resulted from it. There is in fact a tendency to confuse purpose and result, and it is due in part to the ambiguity of the little phrase 'so that' – an ambiguity which, incidentally, is present in the equivalent Greek word (*hina*) also, for it, too, can indicate both purpose and result. Suppose that we read the following sentence: 'The man tinkered with the brakes of his wife's car so that she crashed it when next she used it.' Are we reading about a tragic accident or a crime? Does 'so that' indicate purpose or result? We need to distinguish grammatically between 'so that' meaning 'in order that' and 'so that' meaning 'with the result that', and unless we wish to attribute the child's death to the purpose of God, the two should not be confused. The question we have answered is 'What meaning can we find in this tragedy?' rather than 'Why did it ever happen?' We are not attributing the tragedy to God, but exploring the meaning which God gives to tragedy. There is a sense, then, in which the question '*Why* did this child die?' cannot be answered, except in the sense that we can trace the events that led up to the tragedy; but the question 'Why?' may become unimportant as we discover meaning in the event.

One of the interesting things about the evangelists' treatment of the death of Christ is that they do not have a great deal to say at this deeper level of questioning about the death of Jesus: they attribute it to the wickedness of men and the will of God, but rarely do they spell out what it achieved. Perhaps one explanation of this is that for them the 'answer' to the death of Christ was found first and foremost in the resurrection, for it was the resurrection which transformed the tragedy of Christ's death into triumph and brought sense out of nonsense: it was the resurrection which was the saving event, for here God acted decisively, overthrowing the triumph of evil. Paul sums it up in words taken from Isaiah 25: 'Death is swallowed up in victory'. We are so accustomed to thinking of the death of Christ as itself the saving act of God that we perhaps forget that for the early Christians their first awareness that God was at work in these events came with the resurrection. According to Acts, Peter's first sermon announced that Jesus, who had been killed by the hands of lawless men, had been raised from the dead; in the words of the psalmist, 'Thou wilt not abandon my soul to Hades, nor let thy Holy One see corruption.' Paul defines Christian faith as belief in God who raised Jesus from the dead (Rom. 4.24; 10.9). Here was the event which gave meaning to his death.

And of course, we need to remember that though we tend to speak about the death of Christ (so that it seemed quite natural to choose that phrase as the title for the series of lectures underlying this book) we ought really to be talking of his death and resurrection together. Christians have sometimes concentrated to such an extent on the death of Christ that they almost appear to have forgotten the resurrection, but there would be no point in discussing the cross without belief in the resurrection: that is what gives meaning to his death. And this means that we ought perhaps to pay more attention to the resurrection, to God's vindication of Jesus, than we usually do when we speak about his death.[10]

But if the resurrection is understood as God' act, so, too, is Christ's death. Our writers are unanimous in insisting that Jesus died in accordance with the will of God. They might have explained it otherwise; they might have thought that the crucifixion was such a monstrous crime that it was due entirely to the wickedness of men – that it was an 'accident' which God had to undo. But no! They believed that God was in control of the world, and that what happens there must be seen as part of the divine purpose; moreover, Jesus is his Messiah, and what happens to him cannot be outside God's plan. The death and resurrection of Christ cannot be separated, since both are part of the mysterious purpose of God, and that means that when they began to ask questions about what the death of Jesus achieved, they had no doubt that here, too, they were talking about the purpose of God. What they affirmed was not simply that 'Christ died according to the scriptures,' but that 'Christ died *for our sins* according to the scriptures'.

So there are three important differences between our approach to the contemporary problem about the pointless death of a child and the way in which the early Church answered the question 'Why did Christ die?' First, their problem had at one level received a triumphant solution in

---

10 A recent book by Kenneth Grayston, *Dying, We Live*, London 1990, stresses the importance of thinking of Christ's death and resurrection together. See also D. M. Stanley, *Christ's Resurrection in Pauline Soteriology*, Rome 1961.

the resurrection. Second, they had no hesitation in affirming that Jesus' death had been the will of God. And third, that means that when they went on to the next stage, and began to explore the significance of Christ's death more fully, they were in no doubt that this had been part of God's plan also. Whereas with our explanations of the child's death we wished to distinguish between purpose and result, between 'in order that' and 'with the result that', they saw no need to do so, since they were convinced that it had been God's purpose to reconcile the human race to himself through the death of his Son.

For to say that the meaning of Christ's death is found in the resurrection was, of course, only the beginning of things. What did this victory over death mean? It meant victory for others — victory over death, and over the sin that led to death: in other words, Jesus died 'for' others. It meant a new beginning, a new creation, the establishment of a new people of God. So how did it come about that members of this new community continued to experience pain and suffering — that, indeed, they were persecuted for their faith? Here was another problem that Christians had to think through, as they discovered that it was only *by sharing Christ's suffering* that they could share his victory. The redeemed community learned that those who followed Christ were called to accept his way of life — and death — as a pattern for themselves.

So in different circumstances, and in a variety of images, men and women spelt out the meaning of Christ's death and resurrection, as they tried to express the significance of their experience of God's saving power. They did so in ways that are often different, but by no means incompatible; rather they are complementary, for the truth can never by summed up in one image. Our task in the chapters that follow is to look at the various ways in which our New Testament writers tried to explore the riches of its meaning.

CHAPTER TWO

Paul

We begin our exploration with Paul, because he is our earliest New Testament writer. But of course plenty of things happened before Paul wrote his first letter, and one of the fascinating questions we have to ask in looking at his writings is whether or not it is possible to discover how the gospel was proclaimed before Paul arrived on the scene. Certainly Paul's ways of putting it were not identical with other people's. But to what extent was he a creative thinker? And to what extent did he hand on the tradition that he received? No one who has ever grappled with Paul's writings – and it is no easy task! – can have any doubt that he was an original thinker, a theologian concerned to work out the implications of his new faith; but he was also careful to hand on tradition. The problem is in deciding just where he is being creative, and presenting new insights into the Christian gospel, and where he is handing on the gospel in a form which would be recognized by his fellow-Christians as familiar.

Let us begin by looking at a couple of passages in 1 Corinthians where he reminds his readers of traditions which he has already handed on to them. In chapter 15 he sums up the gospel which he preached to them. It is about Christ, who died for our sins according to the scriptures, who was buried, raised on the third day – again according to the scriptures – and was seen by a long list of witnesses. The problem here is in knowing whether Paul is quoting exactly what he received, or whether he has slipped in a few explanations of his own. A modern writer might put an addition in a footnote, or at least in a bracket, but these options were not available for ancient authors. The fact that Paul begins by stating that he passed on what he received, and ends with the words 'whether it was I or they, so we preached, so you believed', suggests that he is quoting the tradition exactly. But he has certainly made at least one addition to the tradition, by including a statement about his own commissioning as an apostle in the list of witnesses to the resurrection. Has he added anything else? In the course of the summary Paul twice tells us that what happened took place 'in accordance with the scriptures'. It is sometimes suggested that Paul is responsible for this appeal to scripture, but this is something which is stressed by all our New Testament writers, and there is nothing peculiarly Pauline here. Some commentators have suggested that the phrase 'for our sins' is distinctively Pauline and may have been added to the original credal summary. C. H. Dodd, for example, pointed out that in similar summaries in Acts the death of Christ is not specifically linked with forgiveness.[1] But I am inclined to believe that this may be because Luke's summaries probably reflect his understanding of the gospel, and Luke perhaps saw forgiveness of sins as linked with the whole Christ-event, not with the death of Christ alone. There is nothing distinctively Pauline about any of the ideas here. The phrase 'for our sins' contains the word *huper*, meaning 'for', that is used widely in the New Testament in explaining Christ's death.[2] As for the word translated 'sins', *hamartiōn*, Paul himself normally uses this in the singular, to mean the power of sin; two exceptions to this rule – Gal. 1.4 and Col. 1.14 – may well themselves use traditional language. But more important is the fact that almost every other New Testament writer links the forgiveness of sins with the death of Christ. It looks, therefore, as if Paul is doing here exactly what he says he is doing, namely, handing on the tradition which he received: Christ died for our sins according to the scriptures.

The other passage where Paul reminds the Corinthians of the tradition he handed on to them comes in chapter 11. 23–6. This time, he tells us that he received the tradition 'from the Lord'. What does he mean? That he received this tradition about what happened at the Last Supper directly from the Risen Lord? It seems unlikely. This is the kind of story which would have been passed on to him by Peter when they met in Jerusalem.[3] Perhaps he means that the tradition goes right back to the Lord himself – to 'the night on which he was betrayed' – or that it is handed on with the

---

1 *The Apostolic Preaching and its Developments*, London 1936, pp. 7–35.
2 Mark 14.24; John 6.51; 10.15; 11.50; Heb. 2.9; 6.20; 9.24; 10.12.
3 Gal. 1.18; Acts 9.26–8.

Lord's authority, since Jesus commanded the rite to be repeated 'in remembrance' of him. Perhaps he means that the particular *interpretation* which he is giving to what happened at the Last Supper came directly from the Risen Lord – in which case we certainly have a problem in sorting out how much of the tradition is pre-Pauline. In any case, Paul's account is likely to be told in his words and with his emphases and interpretation.

The tradition is about what happened on the night when Jesus was handed over. The usual translation, 'betrayed', disguises the ambiguity in the verb *paradidōmi*. Is Paul referring to the betrayal by Judas? Or is he referring to the 'handing-over' of Jesus to death by God? Paul uses the verb in this second sense in Rom. 4.25 and 8.32, and maybe that is how we should understand it here. Perhaps there is a deliberate ambiguity in the word; we shall find the same ambiguity in the gospels, so there is nothing distinctively Pauline here.

What is the tradition? Jesus took bread, gave thanks, broke it and said 'This is my body, which is for you' – *to huper humōn*. 'For you': there is no verb, though some mss add the word *klōmenon*, 'broken', which seems to be an attempt to spell out what the words mean. Yet perhaps it stresses the wrong point, and the emphasis should rather be on the fact that Jesus' body is 'for you' – that is, to be shared among his disciples. Nor is there any command to eat. We tend to assume that the eating of the bread is all important, but perhaps we are influenced by centuries of Christian practice. Eucharistic theology has concentrated on the bread itself, and interpreted this as 'being' the body of Christ. In Paul's account, it is the action of Jesus in breaking the bread that is central at this point, not the eating, and his words interpret the action: he broke the bread and gave it to them, saying, 'This is my body, which is for you. Do this as my memorial.' What *are* they to do? To break the bread? If so, is it an acted parable? Paul may well have interpreted it as such. Possibly the breaking symbolizes what happens to Jesus' body in death: he is broken – for you; he dies – for you. Or is it the *sharing* that is important – the fact that all eat of the one loaf (1 Cor. 10.17)?

Paul continues: 'in the same way, after supper, the cup'. How can the cup be 'in the same way' as the bread? Does Paul mean that Jesus took up the cup in the same way? That he 'broke' it – in other words, distributed the wine, poured it out? Paul does not in fact say what Jesus did with the cup.

Only that he said 'The cup is the new covenant in my blood.'
The old covenant between God and Israel was sealed with
blood (Ex. 24.8). There was of course no thought of
drinking blood! Nor is there any reference to drinking blood
here; Paul is too much of a Jew for that. The command over
the cup matches that over the bread: they are to 'do this',
whenever they drink, 'as my memorial'. But what are they to
'do'? Since we have not been told what Jesus did with the
cup, it is by no means clear what the disciples are to do! So
we have a double command: the disciples are to 'do this'
(perhaps to break the bread, perhaps to share it) as Jesus'
memorial; and they are to 'do this' with the cup (no action is
specified) whenever they drink, as Jesus' memorial.

Paul's account of what happened at the Last Supper
differs in important respects from the account in the
Synoptic gospels, and it is often argued that his version is
secondary, and that he has altered the tradition found in the
Synoptics which seems to identify the bread with the body
and the wine with the blood. It is sometimes suggested that
he was shying away from the idea, which would have been
abhorrent to a Jew, of drinking blood and eating flesh. Such
arguments seem to suppose that Paul was the only Christian
to be a Jew, and ignore the fact the Jesus himself was Jewish:
the notion of drinking blood would have been equally
impossible for him! If it is true that the Synoptic version of
these words seems to *identify* the wine with the blood, then
it is likely that Paul's version gives us the earlier form of the
words, and that the Synoptic tradition is the more developed.

But we are concerned to see what Paul's summary can tell
us about his understanding of the death of Jesus. As the
conclusion to his summary of the tradition, Paul adds what
is presumably his own interpretation of the meaning of the
celebration of the Lord's Supper in the Christian community: 'As often as you eat this bread and drink this cup, you
proclaim the Lord's death until he comes.' This comment
helps us to understand what Paul means by the term
anamnēsis, which we have been translating in a totally
inadequate way by the word 'memorial'. The English word
suggests simply memory, but in fact the actions of the
eucharist are a proclamation; for the Jews, the Passover is
not simply a remembrance of what took place once, long
ago; it is the re-enactment of those past events in the
present; and it is a looking forward to the final Passover,
when the Messiah will come. For Christians the Lord's

Supper, which was first held at Passover time, is certainly a remembrance of Christ's death, but that means that it is a re-enactment of his death in the present and a looking forward to the time in the future when he comes. This is why eating and drinking this bread and this cup can bring judgement (11.29); the broken bread and poured out wine are symbols of the broken body and poured out blood of the Lord, and those who eat and drink unworthily are guilty of his death.

On the two occasions where Paul tells us that he is quoting tradition, therefore, we have found no evidence to suppose that his basic understanding of the death of Jesus was in fact very different from that of other Christians at the time. But these are not the only passages where Paul may be using traditional summaries about Jesus' death and resurrection. Many scholars argue that there are 'mini' credal statements embedded in his writing. The problem, however, is in knowing how to distinguish between traditional statements which Paul inherited and his own, personal ways of expressing the gospel. Sometimes these passages sound rhythmic and neatly balanced. Might Rom. 4.25, for example, be a traditional couplet? –

> 'He was given up for our trespasses
> and raised for our justification.'

But Paul himself was certainly capable of writing in this way, and the vocabulary sounds thoroughly Pauline. Other passages do contain 'unPauline vocabulary' – that is, words which are not used by Paul elsewhere. An example of this is found in Rom. 3.25, where Paul describes Christ as a *hilastērion* or expiation. Yet the word seems to be an integral part of his argument in this passage; moreover, there are plenty of words and phrases which Paul used on only one occasion in the letters that have come down to us, and we cannot explain them all away as 'borrowed' terms!

Scholars would dearly like to separate out traditional statements from the Pauline letters, because it would enable them to feel that we could know something about the beliefs of other early Christians – of the men and women who believed the gospel before Paul ever wrote to his churches. The fact that we cannot recover such summaries should hardly surprise us, however. We all know how easy it is for new expressions to be forged (perhaps, today, by some politician or television personality) and to become part of everyday language. When we use these expressions it is not because we are consciously quoting, but because they have become part of our own language – we have made them our own. Something similar surely happened with Paul. In the course of this study we shall find various words and ideas reappearing in more than one writer: we have met some of these already in what we *do* know was part of the 'prePauline' tradition – the verb *paradidōmi*, to hand over, the phrase 'for us', the link with the forgiveness of sins, and the idea that Jesus' death and resurrection are parallel to the Passover and Exodus.

It is clear from Paul's letters that the death and resurrection of Jesus are absolutely basic to his faith. Writing to the Corinthians, he reminds them of his message to them: 'I resolved, he says, that I would know nothing while I was among you except Jesus Christ, and him crucified' (2.2) – and we know from 1 Corinthians 15 that this message of 'Christ crucified' included the resurrection! Not surprisingly, a Christian was by definition someone 'for whom Christ died' (1 Cor. 8.11). Paul's message of the cross seemed to many to be foolishness and weakness, but it was in fact about the power and wisdom of God (1 Cor. 1.18–25). Many of the letters begin with a brief summary of the gospel. Thus Rom. 1.3f: 'the gospel is about God's Son . . . he was proclaimed Son of God in power . . . by the resurrection from the dead'. In Galatians, he reminds his readers that the Lord Jesus Christ 'gave himself for our sins, to rescue us from this present evil world' (1.4). 1 Thess. 1.9f. recalls the way in which the Thessalonians responded to his message by turning to God, serving him and 'waiting for his Son to come from heaven – Jesus, who delivers us from the wrath to come'. Always this reminder is phrased in a way appropriate to the situation: the Romans had never met Paul, and needed to be assured that they believed the same gospel; the Corinthians wanted to *add* clever things to the gospel he had brought them; the Galatians had apparently lost faith in Jesus' power to save them from sins and rescue them from this evil age, and the Thessalonians were worried about the future.

We see, then, that Paul does not necessarily always express the message of the cross in the same words, but in ways which speak to the particular needs of those whom he addresses. Sometimes he reminds his readers of what the death and resurrection of Christ have already done for them. This was particularly necessary in writing to the Galatians, who were, in Paul's eyes, in danger of abandoning the gospel altogether (1.6–9; 5.2–4); this gospel, he says, is about

Christ, 'openly displayed on the cross (3.1), whose death has brought them blessing and made them members of God's people. In Romans, he sums up his argument in the statement that all have sinned and all been justified – that is, received the status of righteousness – through God's gracious act of redemption, which took place in Christ's atoning death (Rom. 3.24f.). Once again, we should not suppose that this summary leaves out the resurrection, since 'he was given up for our trespasses, and raised for our justification' (4.25). In Col. 1.13f., Paul[4] describes the way in which we have been brought out of the power of darkness into the kingdom of God's Son, through whom we have redemption and the forgiveness of sins. Gentiles, too, have been made members of God's people (v. 12). The language here reminds us once again of God's redemption of his people at the Exodus. Christ's death is not mentioned but is clearly in mind – and in v. 20 we learn that through his death on the cross all things in heaven and on earth have been reconciled to God. In vv. 21f. the message is brought home to the readers of the letter: you were then alienated from God – but now God has reconciled you in the fleshly body of Christ, through his death.[5]

In this passage (whether by Paul or by someone writing later in Paul's name) we have several ideas that we meet elsewhere in the Pauline letters. The word 'redemption' (*apolutrōsis*), for example, occurs elsewhere, including Rom. 3.24, where it is again linked with the forgiveness of sins.[6] The basic idea underlying the metaphor appears to be that of buying a slave in order to set him or her free. Very similar to this are the verbs *agorazō* (meaning 'to buy'), found in 1 Cor. 6.20 and 7.23, where Paul reminds the Corinthians that they were bought with a price – namely the death of Christ – and *exagorazō* (lit. 'to buy back'), Gal. 3.13; 4.5.

The idea that everything is reconciled to God through

---

4 Many scholars believe that Colossians was not written by the apostle himself, but by a Christian of the next generation, attempting to develop Paul's thinking in relation to the problems of his day. There are, nevertheless, good reasons for maintaining the traditional authorship.

5 Ephesians takes the same idea further. The letter is addressed to Gentiles, who were once 'aliens . . . strangers to the covenant . . . far off'. Now they have been brought near by the blood of Christ: in his flesh he has made Jews and Gentiles one, and has broken down the dividing wall of hostility between them (2.12–14). Ephesians appears to be based on Colossians, and was probably *not* written by Paul.

6 Cf. Eph. 1.7.

Christ's death is also a familiar one in Paul. In Rom. 5.10 he describes the way in which, when we were God's enemies, we were reconciled to him through the death of his Son. Paul sees this reconciliation in global terms: because the Jews failed to respond to the gospel, it has been offered to the Gentiles, and the result has been 'the reconciliation of the world' (Rom. 11.15). The final reconciliation of the Jews when they do at last respond lies in the future.[7] Judging from what Paul says in Rom. 8.19ff. creation itself, subjected to futility and decay because of Adam's sin, will also be restored to harmony. This is certainly the meaning of Col. 1.15–20. But it is in 2 Corinthians 5 that we meet the most extended use of this image of reconciliation. In a passage discussing his own ministry, Paul tells the Corinthians that what compels him to preach is the love of Christ, who died for all (vv. 14f.). Their new life in Christ arises from the fact that they have been reconciled to God. This came about through the initiative of God himself, since God was in Christ, reconciling the world to himself, no longer holding people responsible for their misdeeds. Moreover, he has entrusted this message of reconciliation to Paul and his companions, and he now appeals to the Corinthians through them. So Paul entreats them, on Christ's behalf, to be reconciled to God (vv. 16–20).

There are three interesting things about reconciliation that we can learn from what Paul says here. The first is that, as everywhere else, the initiative lies with God: the gospel is about the gracious activity of God, at work through Christ. The second is that it is *we* who are reconciled to *God* and not *God* to *us*: the gospel is not about placating an angry God, but about an appeal to wayward men and women to be reconciled to a loving Father. The third is that the apostles share in the ministry of reconciliation by addressing the appeal to others.

But if we read on, we find that this 'ministry of reconciliation' involves Paul in more than simply proclaiming the gospel, since in 6.1–10 he describes the sufferings endured by himself and others in the service of the gospel.[8]

---

7 Cf. also Eph. 2.12f., where Gentiles, originally outside the orbit of God's promises, have been brought near through Christ's blood, and Jews and Gentiles have been reconciled to one another.

8 This whole passage is in the plural (until 6.13), so Paul is probably thinking of other preachers besides himself, though it is possible that he is using the 'editorial' plural. His own sufferings are certainly very much in mind.

After listing some of their afflictions, he concludes triumphantly that though they seem to be dying, they are in fact alive; though they appear to be sorrowful, yet they are always rejoicing, though they seem to be poor, yet they make many rich. In this remarkable passage Paul appears to be claiming that he is sharing in a very real way in the death and resurrection of Jesus, participating in his sufferings, and that these sufferings bring benefit to others. It is not so much that he preaches the message of reconciliation as that he embodies it. To understand the basis of this claim we need to look at those passages where Paul spells out his understanding of the significance of the death and resurrection of Christ in terms of 'participation'.

* * *

Let us begin with a simple reference to Christ's death in what is perhaps the earliest of all Paul's letters, 1 Thessalonians. In 5.9f. he urges the Thessalonians not to be scared about what will happen on the Day of the Lord, 'because God has not destined us for wrath, but for salvation, which is obtained through our Lord Jesus Christ, who died for us, so that whether we wake or sleep we might live with him.' Paul is looking forward here to the final day of judgement; 'you Christians, he declares, have no cause for concern, because your fate has already been decided. You are destined for salvation, because Christ died for you.' The death of Jesus somehow works 'for' Christians, on their behalf, to save them from future wrath. How does it work? How does Christ's death save us from wrath? The only clue that Paul gives us here is that 'he died for us, so that whether we wake or sleep we might live with him'. The reference to waking or sleeping is meant to reassure those Thessalonians who are worried about dying before the Day of the Lord arrives; it makes no difference, says Paul, whether you are dead or alive on the final day, because Christ died for us in order that we might live with him.

Christ died for us. What is Paul saying here? Some commentators have assumed that Paul is thinking of Christ's death here as substitutionary.[9] But this does not seem to me to be an appropriate way of describing it. For one thing, Christ's death does not eliminate the possibility of our own physical death; maybe the Thessalonians thought that it did,

---

9 E.g. L. Morris, *The Cross in the Pauline Epistles*, Grand Rapids 1965, Exeter 1976, p. 225.

and maybe this is why they were disturbed when some of their number fell ill and died, but Paul is certainly aware that Jesus' death does not prevent our own; we may be awake or we may sleep – in that respect, the death of Jesus makes no difference. Nor (as we shall discover later) does the fact of Jesus' death eliminate the necessity for our dying *with* Jesus. Moreover, the second part of Paul's sentence makes it clear that the idea of substitution is inadequate. A friend of mine died under the wheels of a bus, saving the life of a child; her death can truly be described as substitutionary, since she died in order that the child might live. But notice what Paul writes: *not* 'Christ died, in order that we might live,' but 'Christ died, in order that we might live *with him*'. The life we live through Christ's self-sacrifice comes not only from his dying, but from his living again: he has been raised from the dead, and we share that resurrection life. It is not, then, a question of Christ and the believer exchanging places; it is rather a sharing of experiences. Christ died, and we live with him.

We turn now to Galatians, another of Paul's early letters, and one in which the cross is central to Paul's argument. Christ's death is mentioned in the opening line, where Paul spells out his credentials: his commission comes from Jesus Christ and God the Father, who raised him from the dead. Immediately after the greeting Paul gives a summary of the gospel, as though to remind the Galatians – who have apparently forgotten! – just what this is. Our Lord Jesus Christ gave himself for our sins to rescue us from the present evil age, according to the will of our God and Father. Once again, we are on familiar ground: we recognize familiar themes – so also, presumably, would the Galatians. Jesus died for our sins – *huper tōn hamartiōn hēmōn*: the words are the same as Paul uses in 1 Corinthians 15. He died to rescue us from this present age; the language is somewhat unusual in Paul, but the idea is similar to the one we have just looked at in 1 Thessalonians, for this present evil age stands in contrast to the future age, which follows the Day of the Lord. He died according to the will of our God and Father; in 1 Corinthians 15 it was according to the scriptures – which set out the will of God. Christ's death, then, is no accident, but part of God's plan for mankind's redemption. Finally, we notice the opening words: 'Christ gave himself'. Here we meet a new idea; whereas in our other summaries, we have been told simply that Christ died, or that he was given up or handed over, now we learn that he gave himself.[10] In other words, Paul sees Christ as playing an active role in mankind's redemption; Christ is not simply the victim but the willing participant in his death. Notice how these brief statements deal with the problems connected with Christ's death which we looked at in the last chapter. Jesus was not a criminal, punished for his own crimes – on the contrary, he suffered for the sins of others; nor was he a blasphemer – rather, he gave himself up in accordance with the will of God, much as the Maccabean martyrs had died because of their obedience to God's law. And we have positive interpretation also, discovering meaning in his death: it was 'for our sins'; and it was 'to rescue us from this present evil age'.

Paul spells out this meaning further in the following chapter, where he is arguing about how men and women are justified – that is, brought into a right relationship with God; this relationship is not created, he says, on the basis of the works of the law, but on the basis of the obedient death of Christ, 'who loved me and gave himself for me' (2.20). Notice how, once again, Paul is thinking of Christ as a willing participant in his own death; once again we have the verb *paradidōmi*, but this time with Christ himself as the subject – perhaps we should translate these words as 'who loved me and handed himself over for me'. But what is the result of Christ's love and self-sacrifice? As in 1 Thessalonians, it is life for the believer – and as there, it is totally inadequate to suggest that Christ dies *instead of* men and women. This time Paul spells out the fact that Christ's death involves ours: 'for through the law I have died to the law,' he says; in other words, the judgement pronounced by the law on Christ included Paul himself. 'I have been crucified with Christ.' Christ's death for us involves us in dying with him. He died as our representative, on our behalf. But the life which follows is also shared. I died, says Paul, 'in order that I might live to God'. But what sort of life is this? 'It is no longer I who live, but Christ who lives in me; the life I now live in the flesh I live by faith in the Son of God' – or, as we perhaps ought to translate it, 'the life I now live I live through the faithfulness of the Son of God'.[11] Either way, it

---

10 The verb used here is *didōmi*. In 1 Cor. 11.23, Rom. 4.25 and 8.32 it is *paradidōmi*.

11 The phrase *pistis Christou*, 'faith in Christ', can be understood as either a subjective genitive (Christ's faith/faithfulness) or an objective genitive (faith in Christ). Most translators and commentators have assumed in the past that the latter understanding was correct, but recently

seems to be a case of Christ taking over our lives and living in our place. So, then, it is by dying with Christ that the Christian shares in Christ's resurrection; and it is by sharing that resurrection that the Christian is pronounced righteous.

In chapter 3, Paul launches a bitter attack on the Galatians. They wish to accept circumcision, but in doing so they are in his view accepting the law and all its demands; that means that obedience to the law will be the basis of their relationship with God. If this is the way to justification, says Paul, then Christ died to no purpose and the Galatians have in effect abandoned the gospel. Hence Paul's cry of anguish in 3.1: 'You fools! – Before whose eyes Jesus Christ was publicly placarded as crucified.' The force of Paul's language is felt only when we remember the degradation of the cross, and the humiliation involved in displaying the naked body of the victim in public. Paul makes no attempt to disguise the scandal, which adds force to his question: what was the point of Christ's death if one can be justified by obedience to the law?

He backs up his argument by appealing, first of all, to the Galatians' own experience: they received the Spirit of God – knew themselves to be children of God – when they believed the Gospel, not when they obeyed the law. Secondly, by quoting scripture, and showing that the principle that one is justified by faith goes right back to Abraham, with whom the original covenant was made. So far so good. But Paul has not yet said anything to explain why the death of Christ is *necessary*. After all, Abraham believed in God – and that sufficed. If Abraham believed God and was justified, why was it necessary for Christ to die?

It is important to understand that Paul's argument starts from the fact of the cross. The death of Christ has to be explained – and in the process of explanation, it becomes that which explains everything else. Paul would never have argued that the law could not work unless he had had to explain the cross. As a Jew, it never occurred to him to question that God's relationship with Israel was based on his

---

more and more scholars have argued for the former. See especially G. Howard, 'The "Faith of Christ" ', *Exp. Tim.* 85, 1974, p. 213, 'On the "Faithfulness of Christ" ', *HTR* 60, 1967, pp. 459–65; R. B. Hays, *The Faith of Christ*, Chico, 1983. It is possible that the phrase contains both meanings: see Sam K. Williams, 'Again Pistis Christou', *CBQ* 49, 1987, pp. 431–47, M. D. Hooker, '*Pistis Christou*', *NTS* 35, 1989, pp. 321–42, reprinted in *From Adam to Christ*, Cambridge 1990, pp. 165–86.

covenant with her, and that this covenant included the nation's obedience to the law. But Christ's death made him think again about the role of the law, and led him to the conclusion that the cross invalidates the law as the basis of this relationship between men and women and God. For either one must accept the verdict of the law – according to which the manner of Jesus' death demonstrates that he was a sinner and a blasphemer – or one must accept the verdict of the resurrection, which demonstrates that Jesus was in fact approved and vindicated by God. In Paul's view, one cannot have it both ways: one must face up to the scandal of the cross, and realize its implications. If one accepts the gospel, and believes that Jesus has been declared to be God's Son by his resurrection from the dead (Rom. 1.3f.), then one must recognize that the Jewish law had built-in obsolescence; since the verdict of the law on Jesus has been overthrown, the law itself has been nullified.

But there was another reason that led Paul to rethink the question of the basis of the relationship between God and his people. He has preached the gospel to Gentiles – including the Galatians – and they have responded and believed his message. The gift of the Holy Spirit proves that these Gentiles have been acknowledged by God as his children; but this means that it is no longer necessary to be a Jew in order to belong to God's people – no longer necessary, therefore, to be circumcised and to obey the law. Jews assumed that in order to be a child of God it was necessary to be a child of Abraham;[12] Paul agrees – but argues that being a child of Abraham means sharing his faith, not being his literal descendant.

But why is the death of Christ the basis of this new relationship? In Gal. 3.10–14 Paul spells out his answer in some of the most obscure verses in the whole New Testament. First, he tells us that the law, far from leading to righteousness, brings a curse to everyone who does not obey it; secondly, he demonstrates from scripture that righteousness is in fact based on faith, not law; and thirdly, he tells us that Christ redeems us from the curse of the law by himself becoming a curse, as Deut. 21.23 says. Finally, he declares that as a result, the blessing of Abraham has come on the

---

12 The phrases Paul uses are 'sons of God' and 'sons of Abraham'. Gal. 3.26, 7. The reason is obvious: not only was inheritance through the male line, but in Judaism, the greatest privileges belonged to *male* descendants of Abraham.

Gentiles, and that we have all received the promised Spirit of God – we are all his children.

Paul here faces squarely up to the scandal of the cross. He accepts the judgement of Deut. 21.23. But he has a problem. If Christ did indeed become a curse, how is it that he has proved to be a source of blessing? How is it that through his death we have received, not a curse, but blessing and promise? Paul's answer is that the promise made to Abraham of future blessing was in fact made to Christ. He argues that the promise was made to Abraham and to his offspring, and that because the word for 'offspring' (*sperma*) is singular, this must refer to one person, namely to Christ. The blessing and the promise should, then, have come to him. So how is it that they have come to others? How is it that Gentiles have shared in the blessing promised to Abraham, and that Christians, both Jews and Gentiles, have received the Spirit of God? The answer is that Christians are 'in Christ'; it is because they are united with him that they share his blessing, his sonship; like him, they are children of Abraham – members of God's holy nation, and in a right relationship with him.

But there seems to be a vital piece of information missing! In Gal. 3.14 Paul jumps, without explanation, from his statement that Christ was made a curse to the affirmation that Gentiles have received the blessing. How does one lead to the other? Again, some commentators have interpreted this in substitutionary terms; they have suggested that Christ and the believer exchange places.[13] Paul's answer is, I believe, far more profound. But in order to understand his position it is essential to grasp the importance for him of the union between Christ and the believer. It is 'in Christ Jesus' – in union with him – that we experience the blessing and receive the promise (3.14). Once again, we are reminded of those words in 1 Thess. 5.10 – Christ died, in order that we might live with him; if blessing comes to us, it is because we are in him; if we receive the Spirit, it is because we share his life – and as we shall discover in chapter 4 the Spirit we receive is in fact the Spirit of the Son. It is not, then, a case of Christ and the believer changing places, but of the believer sharing in Christ's life. If Christ has been vindicated and raised from the dead, the same must be true of those who are united with him.

Strangely, however, Paul appears to have missed a stage

13 L. Morris, *op. cit.*, p. 222f.

out of the argument. The blessing comes to us because we are in Christ, the Spirit is the Spirit of the living Son – but Paul has said nothing about the resurrection! In fact the last thing he told us about Christ is that he was impaled on a cross, under a curse. Now it is quite clear that Paul's argument depends on the resurrection; without the resurrection, there can be no thought of believers being 'in Christ', no question of blessing or promise being received by anyone. Moreover it was the resurrection which vindicated Jesus and which showed that the verdict of the law upon him was wrong; he had been falsely put to death, and the curse was therefore null and void. The power of the curse has somehow been absorbed, contained, and blessing has been let loose, rather like nuclear waste which is (hopefully) safely imprisoned in a concrete bunker when energy has been released. All this, I believe, is implied in Paul's argument. If he does not mention the resurrection specifically, perhaps it is because this seemed obvious. After all, the resurrection itself is not specifically mentioned in 1 Thessalonians 5: 'Christ died for us, so that we might live with him.' The resurrection is presupposed.

There is another important point regarding this profound passage in Galatians 3 that we must note before we leave it. It is this: we have spoken of Christian experience as a sharing in the risen life of Christ, but Gal. 3.13 reminds us of the other side of the equation, and this is that Christ shares in our human life. The curse belonged, not to him, but to us; the death he died was *our* death. Christ shared our humanity, our estrangement from God, in order that we might share his sonship, his relationship with God.

Let us turn now to another passage which is in many ways very similar to Gal. 3.13 – and equally difficult. In 2 Cor. 5.21 we find the startling comment: 'For our sake God made Christ to be sin who knew no sin, so that in him we might become the righteousness of God.' What can Paul mean by the statement that Christ was made sin? Once again, some commentators interpret it in substitutionary terms;[14] others, perplexed by Paul's blunt language, attempt to explain it as a reference to the sin-offering of the Old Testament. When Paul says that Christ was made *hamartia*, they argue, he means, not that he was made sin, but that he was made into a sin-offering. But the Old Testament phrase for this is *peri hamartias*, not *hamartia*, and this explanation looks very

---

14 L. Morris, *op. cit.*, p. 220f.

much like clutching at straws. Once again, Paul is emphasizing the scandal of the cross; paradoxical though it may be, in the eyes of the law the Messiah was there branded as a sinner – though in fact, Paul is careful to explain, he was without sin.

The structure of the sentence is beginning to seem familiar. Once again, what happened was *huper hēmōn* – 'for us'. In what sense was it 'for us'? Paul explains that it happened 'in order that' we might become the righteousness of God in Christ. Compare with this the other passages we have looked at:

Christ died, in order that we might live with him (1 Thess. 5.10).

Christ became a curse, in order that in Christ Jesus blessing might come on the Gentiles (Gal. 3.13).

Now we learn that Christ was made sin, in order that we might become the righteousness of God in him (2 Cor. 5.21).

Paul has now given us three statements that the death of Christ took place in order that something might happen to us; three sets of opposites – *death leads to life, curse leads to blessing, sin leads to righteousness.* Christ shared our condition of sin and alienation and death in order that we might share his victory. We can find other examples of sayings of this kind in Paul, though they seem to be about what we would call 'incarnation' rather than 'atonement': later in 2 Corinthians Paul urges the Corinthians to contribute to the collection for the poor (2 Cor. 8.9); why should they? 'Because Christ became poor for your sake, in order that you might become rich.' In Gal. 4.4f., we are told that God sent his Son, born under the law, born under a woman, in order that we might be set free from the law and made sons of God. In the second century, Irenaeus was to sum this up in one memorable sentence: '*Christ became what we are in order that we might become what he is.*'[15] Death, life; curse, blessing; law, liberty; slavery, sonship; sin, righteousness; riches, poverty. These bold sentences express Paul's conviction that Christ shares fully in the human situation in order that, *in him*, we may share in his.

How does this come about? How do we become the righteousness of God in him? Once again, we must assume that it is by the resurrection. When Christ is raised from the dead he is vindicated, declared to be righteous. If we become the righteousness of God in him it is because those who are

---

15 *Adv. Haer.* V *praef.*

in him share his righteousness.[16] And though Paul does not specifically say so in 2 Cor. 5.21, it is clear enough from the context that it is through the resurrection that we 'become righteousness in him'. Indeed, the context helps us to see a little more clearly how Paul understands the death of Christ to 'work'. In 2 Cor. 5.14 he writes: 'We are convinced that one has died for all'. 'For all' – that little word *huper* once again. What does this 'for all' mean? It means, says Paul, that all have died. *Christ died, not instead of the human race, but as their representative*: in some mysterious sense, the whole of humanity died on Calvary. Moreover, he died 'for all, in order that those who live might no longer live for themselves, but for him who for their sake died and was raised'. Paul's interpretation of what the death of Christ involves reminds us of his words in Gal. 2.20. He dies for us; but that means that we die *with* him. He was raised, and raised with such power that our lives are now taken over by him. No wonder Paul describes it as a new creation (2 Cor. 5.17); with the death and resurrection of Christ, the old way of life has been swept away, and a new one inaugurated. This is why Christ is for us 'righteousness and sanctification and redemption' (1 Cor. 1.30), and if we ask, 'how do *we* become righteous?' the answer is that we have been 'washed, sanctified and justified (or made righteous) in the name of the Lord Jesus Christ' (1 Cor. 6.11).[17]

But if we are to understand what Paul means by this talk about old and new we must turn to Romans 5. Once again, we find him using the word *huper*, meaning 'for' or 'on behalf of'. Christ died 'for the ungodly,' he says; he died 'for us' (vv. 6 and 8). Vv. 12–21 help us to understand something of what he means by those statements, for even though Christ's death is not specifically mentioned, it is in fact the key to understanding those verses. Paul here compares and contrasts what happened through Adam and what happened through Christ: through Adam came sin and death, he says; and since all men and women are 'in Adam' – that is, they share the weakness of humanity – they all sin, and they all die. But through Christ come righteousness and life, and those who are in him share his righteousness and

---

16 Cf. John Wesley's translation of the words of Nicholaus von Zinzendorf:

'Jesu, Thy blood and righteousness
My beauty are, my glorious dress.

17 For similar ideas, see Col. 1.22; Eph. 1.4; 5.25ff.

life. Adam – Christ, sin – righteousness, death – life: one
might think that Paul had nicely-balanced opposites. But he
insists that they do *not* balance; and the reason they do not
balance is that what happens in Christ is the work of God;
in Christ we are confronted by the grace of God. The
judgement which pronounced condemnation on mankind is
as nothing beside the free gift of God which offers
reconciliation. If death came into the world because of one
man's trespass, how much more will life reign abundantly
through the one man Jesus Christ. The argument is summed
up in vv. 18–19: one man's trespass led to condemnation for
everyone; similarly, one man's acquittal[18] led to righteousness of life for everyone; one man's disobedience made
everyone a sinner; similarly, one man's obedience will make
everyone righteous.

Notice familiar themes: Christ dies 'for us'. Paul attributes
Christ's actions to the grace of God and the grace of Christ,
and speaks repeatedly of what happens as 'gift' or as
'gracious gift', and we remember that we were told elsewhere that God gave Christ up, or that he gave himself up.
In this passage Paul stresses the obedience of Christ. In
marked contrast to Adam, who was disobedient, Christ was
obedient to God's will; this is why he is able to reverse
Adam's sin and why life proves more powerful than death.
Finally, we notice that Paul's understanding of how Christ's
death 'works' depends on the notion of human solidarity.
Just as we are united in our common humanity by our
weakness and sin and subjection to death, so now we can be
united in a new humanity – one that is marked by power, by
righteousness and by life. This understanding is based on
Paul's belief that what happens to Christ has a fundamental
effect on the standing of men and women before God.

What Paul is setting out here is one of his most basic ways
of interpreting what takes place through the death and
resurrection of Christ – the interpretation that is normally
known as 'justification'. Unfortunately this term does not
convey Paul's meaning adequately, and English lacks the
words to do so. The idea is rooted in the righteousness
(*dikaiosunē*) of God – a word which means not simply
'uprightness' but the activity that puts right what is wrong.
God himself is righteous (*dikaios*), and demands righteous-

---

18 The case for this translation is argued in M. D. Hooker, 'Interchange
and Atonement', *B.J.R.L.* 60, 1978, pp. 462–81, reprinted in *From Adam
to Christ*, pp. 26–41.

ness from his people. His righteousness was expected in the salvation of his people – and is demonstrated, so Paul says, in his salvation of the ungodly, who are thereby 'justified' (*dikaioō*) – brought into a right relationship with himself, and given the status of those who are righteous. For centuries, theologians argued as to whether sinners were *made* righteous or were *treated* as righteous when they were not.[19] The answer to this conundrum is to be found in Paul's idea that believers possess a 'solidarity' in Adam and in Christ. This means that just as those 'in Adam' share his sin, so now those who are 'in Christ' share his status – his righteousness before God (Rom. 8.1; 1 Cor. 1.30), and even the sonship conferred on him at the resurrection (Rom. 1.4; 8.14–17; Gal. 3.26f.). Because he was vindicated at the resurrection, those who are 'in him' are also vindicated, or 'justified': just as they shared the judgement on Adam, so now they enjoy the gift of righteousness which belongs to those who are in Christ (Rom. 5.17).

But in order to grasp the significance of Paul's understanding of what Christ's death means, we must read on in Romans to chapter 6. To be sure, he is here discussing the theme of baptism. But Christian baptism is baptism into the death and resurrection of Christ, and what it entails is nothing less than death and resurrection for the believer: death to the old life – life lived in Adam – death to sin, and resurrection to a new life in Christ. In baptism, Christians are plunged into Christ; they *share* his death, they *share* his resurrection. This is the heart of Paul's understanding of the relationship between Christ and the believer. Christ is the representative man – the new Adam. By joining ourselves to him, men and women share his obedience – an obedience which led him to death – and they share his vindication, in resurrection. That is why they have died to the old life of sin, and why they embark on a new life of righteousness. Once slaves to sin, they are now slaves to righteousness – a hopelessly inadequate image which Paul abandons, preferring instead to talk about our sonship. So once again we see that Christians become what Christ is: God sent his Son, in the likeness of sinful flesh and for sin; as a result, men and women become children of God and fellow heirs with Christ (8.1–17).

There is another passage where Paul spells out the

19 See, for example, the classic study of J. Ziesler, *The Meaning of Righteousness in Paul*, Cambridge 1972.

meaning of Christ's obedience: it is Philippians 2. Christ
emptied himself, took the form of a slave, shared the likeness
of men, humbled himself, and was obedient to death – even
to death on a cross. There was no need to remind the
Philippians that death on a cross was appropriate for a slave,
since crucifixions were likely to have been all too familiar. It
is worth noticing two things in this passage, both of which
we have met before. The first is the way in which Christians
are called to share Christ's obedience and his death. Paul
concludes the passage with this appeal to the Philippians: 'so
then, as you have always obeyed, do so now' (v. 12), and in
the following chapter he describes how he himself has given
up everything for the sake of Christ, and how he is willing to
share his sufferings and to be conformed to his death (3.7–
10). Christ shares our human lot, accepts the most scan-
dalous of human deaths; and we in turn are called to share
in his self-giving and in his death. The second is what results.
For Christ, the outcome was vindication, exaltation and the
proclamation of his Lordship (2.9–11); for those who are
found in him it is the righteousness which belongs to him
(3.9); and because we share his righteousness we have the
hope of sharing in his resurrection, the promise that we shall
be transformed to be like him (3.10f., 21).[20]

* * *

The idea that Christians are called on to share in the
sufferings of Christ, in hope of sharing his resurrection, is
one that we shall meet again; in the Gospels, for example,
would-be disciples are challenged to deny themselves, to
shoulder their crosses and to follow Jesus, and are promised
final vindication before God by the Son of man.[21] But Paul's
letters are clearly written by someone who has *experienced*
suffering in the service of his master. He knows what it
means to renounce his privileges (Phil. 3.7f.) and to endure
suffering (v. 10) – just as Jesus himself renounced his unique
privilege[22] and endured suffering.[23] In Gal. 6.17 he describes
himself as bearing the marks of Jesus branded on his body.
The word used here, *stigmata*, came to be used in later times

---

20 Many of the ideas in this chapter are explored in greater depth in
From Adam to Christ.
21 E.g. Mark 8.34,38.
22 Phil. 2.6–8.
23 Paul used the verb *hēgeomai* (translated 'regard' or 'count' in NRSV
and REB) three times in Phil. 3.7f. – the same verb that he uses in 2.6 of
Christ.

of the wounds of Jesus, but in Paul's day the term was used of the marks of ownership branded onto slaves: the scars that Paul has acquired in the course of his ministry are thus an indication that he belongs to Christ (Gal. 1.10).

But it is in 2 Corinthians that he speaks in greatest detail of his sufferings in the service of Christ. He spells these out in two remarkable passages. First, in 4.7–12, he insists that he is not defeated by his[24] afflictions, since although he is always carrying about the death of Jesus in his body, this is in order that the life of Jesus may be revealed in him as well. Then comes the remarkable conclusion: 'so death is at work in us, *but life in you*'. The second passage, in 6.4–10, as we saw earlier,[25] makes a similar point. Paul lists the many sufferings that have come his way – yet in death he is alive, in sorrow he is rejoicing, and though he is poor he makes many rich. This is precisely what he describes Jesus himself as doing two chapters later (8.9). Conformity to the sufferings of Christ means that, in some mysterious way, the redeeming grace of Christ works *through* him. As he puts it in his opening doxology, he is able in all his afflictions to console others, because although the sufferings of Christ 'abound' in his case, so does the consolation that comes through Christ – which means that he is afflicted 'for' the Corinthians' consolation and salvation; and they in turn share in both the affliction and the consolation (2 Cor. 1.3–7). Twice in v. 6 he uses the little word *huper*, 'for', which he uses when describing what Christ's death does 'for us'. In all these passages, Paul is claiming that because he shares the sufferings of Christ, he experiences also the power of his resurrection – and, even more significant, that he becomes a channel whereby this resurrection life is passed on to others.

An even more striking expression of this idea is found in Col. 1.24, where Paul describes himself as rejoicing in his sufferings 'for you', and writes: 'I am completing, for the sake of Christ's body, the Church, what is lacking – as far as I am concerned – in his sufferings.' This translation is an attempt to deal with a major problem of interpretation, since

---

24 All these passages are in the plural; Paul is not alone in suffering for the sake of the gospel – though precisely who else is included we do not know. Presumably Timothy, who joins Paul in sending the letter, 1.1, is among them.

25 Above, pp.25f.

the passage is often translated as though the apostle were claiming that he was completing what was lacking in Christ's sufferings.[26] Paul – or whoever else wrote Colossians (a letter which emphasizes the superiority of Christ) – could certainly never have suggested that anything was lacking in Christ's own sufferings, or in his ability to redeem others! But we have seen elsewhere that Paul believed himself to be sharing in Christ's sufferings, and that since his sufferings arose in the course of his endeavours to spread the gospel, there was a very real sense in which his afflictions brought comfort to others (2 Cor. 1.3–7). Since he also believed himself to be called to the task of evangelism, he may well have felt that he had been allocated a particular quota of Christ's sufferings: if he is to complete this task of proclaiming Christ (Col. 1.28f.), he must also complete his share of suffering.

In the passages we have looked at in 2 Corinthians, Paul speaks of participation in the death and resurrection of Jesus as a present experience. But Paul was not yet dead, and if bodily death was still a future prospect, so was bodily resurrection. His present experiences were only a foretaste of what was still to come. So his account of what it means to be constantly given up to death for Jesus' sake leads into the declaration that 'We know that the one who raised the Lord Jesus will raise us also with him' (2 Cor. 4.14). Similarly, in Phil. 3.10, he describes himself as sharing in the sufferings and death of Jesus in hope of sharing also in the resurrection, and in Rom. 8.17 he assures the Romans that if they suffer with Christ now, they will be glorified with him in the future.

And just as their present experience of sharing Christ's suffering means that Christians can confidently look forward to sharing his resurrection, so baptism into Christ's death is an assurance of the life to come. 'If we have been identified with him in a death like his, we shall also be identified with him in his resurrection' (Rom. 6.5). This resurrection lies in the future, yet it already spills over into the present, because

---

26 See W. F. Flemington, 'On the interpretation of Colossians 1:24', in *Suffering and Martyrdom in the New Testament*, edd. William Horbury and Brian McNeil, Cambridge 1981, who argues that the phrase 'in my flesh', here paraphrased as 'as far as I am concerned', belongs closely to 'what is lacking in the sufferings of Christ'.

there is a very real sense in which Christians have already begun a new life in Christ. This experience is expressed in different ways. Because of Christ's resurrection, those who have died with Christ in baptism have set out on a new life (Rom. 6.4). Those who are crucified with Christ have died to the law in order to live to God, but now in fact it is Christ who lives in them rather than they themselves (Gal. 2.19f.). Christ died for all, so that those who live should no longer live for themselves, but for him who for their sake died and was raised to life: the quality of this new life is such that it can be described as 'a new creation' (2 Cor. 5.15, 17).

This sharing in the death and resurrection of Christ – in the past (in baptism), in the present (in suffering, and in a new manner of life) or in the future (in final acceptance and vindication) – is all part of Paul's understanding of Christ's solidarity with humanity, expressed in Romans 5 and in 1 Corinthians 15. His death and resurrection are the bridge between the old age and the new, since those who are baptized into Christ share his death to the old age, and begin again in the new. As long as they continue life on this planet, they continue to share the weakness of Adam, but at the Last Day they will exchange the likeness of Adam for the likeness of Christ (1 Cor. 15.42–9). Paul's whole argument in 1 Corinthians 15 regarding the future resurrection of Christians is based on the affirmation that Jesus died and was raised again. He sums it up again in 2 Cor. 4.14, where he says that the God who raised the Lord Jesus will raise us too. Elsewhere he argues *from* the death and resurrection of Christ *to* the future with a triumphant 'how much more':

'If God showed his love for us in the fact that Christ died for us while we were sinners, how much more, being "justified" by his blood, shall we be saved through him from wrath.

'And if, while we were enemies, we were reconciled to God through the death of his Son, how much more, being reconciled, shall we be saved by his life' (Rom. 5.8–10).

A similar argument is found in 1 Thessalonians, where Paul assures his readers that since God raised Jesus from the dead, they can confidently expect him to save them from wrath (1 Thess. 1.10; 4.14; 5.9f.). If Jesus' death is a demonstration of God's love for us, his resurrection is a guarantee that we shall be saved – because of our union with him.

But what is this wrath from which we are saved? It is, of course, the wrath of God himself – divine punishment for human rebellion and sin. Paul's description of God's wrath[27] has led some scholars to the conclusion that Paul thinks of Christ's death as a 'propitiation'.[28] The problem with this particular word is that it suggests, first, that it is possible for men and women to 'propitiate' God, and second, that an angry God is turned by Christ's death into a forgiving God. If one thing is clear from Paul's writings it is that the initiative in dealing with sin and reconciling men and women to himself lies with God, whose purpose and plan is their salvation. Certainly his wrath will be poured out on those who refuse to repent – but for those who *do* repent God provides a means of dealing with their sins, and so of averting wrath. In Rom. 3.24f., Paul sets out God's remedy for the situation of universal sin he has described in chs. 1– 3. God's righteousness has now been revealed (3.21f.) – not in wrath, but in redemption! 'Everyone has sinned, and . . . is justified, freely, by God's grace, through the redemption which is in Christ Jesus – whom God put forward as an atoning sacrifice, by his death, through faith'. The term *hilastērion*, here translated 'an atoning sacrifice', *can* mean 'propitiation', but in the LXX (i.e. the Greek translation of the Old Testament) the verb from which it is derived (*hilaskesthai*) is used to translate the Hebrew *kipper*, meaning 'to cover over', 'wipe off' or 'cleanse'; this is what the sin-offerings were intended to do – wipe away sins. The noun *hilastērion* itself is used to translate *kappōret*, the Hebrew word used of the lid which covered the Ark of the Covenant, sometimes referred to as 'the mercy seat'. Since it is God who 'put forward' Jesus, the translation 'propitiation' certainly seems inappropriate here; 'expiation' is better, suggesting that (as in the cult) God has provided in Christ's death a sin-offering that can wipe away sin. But perhaps Paul is using the word *hilastērion* in its LXX sense, to mean 'mercy seat'[29] – that is the *place* of expiation where the high priest sprinkled blood on the Day of Atonement.

Paul is clearly describing Christ's death in sacrificial terms,

---

27 See especially Rom. 1.18–3.20.
28 L. Morris, *The Atonement: Its Meaning and Significance*, Leicester, 1983.
29 As in Heb. 9.5, the only other place in the New Testament where the term is used.

but is he thinking of the lamb whose blood wipes away the sins of the people, or does he have in mind the mercy seat, the place where atonement – reconciliation – is made?[30] It may well be that the answer is 'both', and that Jesus is here seen both as the atoning sacrifice *and* as the place where God and humanity are reconciled; we shall find similar attempts by the authors of the Fourth Gospel and of Hebrews to apply more than one image at a time to Jesus.[31] In any case, it seems probable that Paul has the ritual of the Day of Atonement in mind, since the sin-offering sacrificed on that day was meant to deal with the sins of all Israel; now, in the death of Jesus, God has provided a much greater sin-offering, the answer to the sins of Jews and Gentiles alike.[32]

Nor are these the only sacrificial images that Paul uses. A striking one occurs in 1 Cor. 5.7, where he writes: 'Christ our Passover is crucified for us'. The image is highly appropriate, since the Passover was celebrated at the same time of year as the Festival of Unleavened Bread, and Paul is here urging the Corinthians to get rid of the 'old leaven' of immorality which has no place in their new life in Christ. We have seen elsewhere that Christ's death and resurrection inaugurate a new situation which does away with the old.[33] In Rom. 8.3, he describes Christ as being sent by God 'for sin'. The phrase may mean simply 'to deal with sin', but possibly we should understand it to mean 'as an offering for sin', since the Greek (*peri hamartias*) is sometimes used in that sense in the LXX. But if so, it seems to be thrown in almost as an afterthought to the main theme, which is the familiar one that Christ was born as man ('in the likeness of sinful man'), in order that we might become children of God (8.15–23).

---

30 So T. W. Manson, *JTS* xlvi, 1945, pp. 1–10.
31 In John 1.29, 36, Jesus is described as the Lamb who takes away the sins of the world; this seems to be a combination of various different Old Testament lambs. In Heb. 9.11–14, Jesus is both the sacrificial victim and the high priest who offers the sacrifice.
32 A similar idea is developed later by the author of Hebrews.
33 E.g. Romans 6. Cf. also 1 Cor. 6.11.

Paul uses a variety of images in speaking about the cross. There are others which we have not considered – notably, the idea that in Christ's death the powers of darkness were defeated.[34] None of them is complete in itself, for there is no one way of fathoming the riches of this theme. It would be foolish to think that we had understood all that Paul has to say, let alone the significance of the event itself. If we have concentrated in this chapter on the idea of participation in the death and resurrection of Christ, it is because it appears to be of special importance for Paul. Because Christ dies as our representative, our status before God is changed and a new situation is brought about. Christians share his death, and they share his life, but because the life they now lead is *his* life, it must be conformed to his.

When Paul sets out to expound his understanding of the gospel to the Romans, he introduces his exposition with the comment 'I am not ashamed of the gospel' (1.16). He might well have been! The almost defensive tone suggests that opponents have mocked his gospel, and that even some of his converts were ashamed of it: they shied away from the absurd 'gospel' about a crucified felon. But Paul is far from being ashamed of it – he glories in it, 'for it is the power of God leading to salvation' and turns all human values upside down. Failure to grasp this, as we saw in chapter 1, lay at the heart of the problem in Corinth, where Paul's converts had clearly not begun to see that good news based on a cross carried certain implications about their own life-style. Those who proclaim modern travesties of the gospel, which promise ease and health and wealth, also need to heed Paul's warning against those who live as enemies of the cross of Christ. Those who accept this shameful gospel, and who are willing to identify themselves with Christ's crucifixion and

---

34 See, in particular, the suggestion that the rulers of this world brought about their own destruction by crucifying Jesus in 1 Cor. 2.8; the references to the 'elemental spirits of the universe' from whom we have been rescued in Gal. 4.3 and Col. 2.8, 20; the statement that in the cross God disarmed the principalities and powers and triumphed over them, Col. 2.15; and the various references to Christ ruling over all other powers and authorities, Rom. 8.38f.; 1 Cor. 15.24–6; Phil. 2.10; Eph. 1.21f. For a discussion of this theme see G. B. Caird, *Principalities and Powers*, Oxford 1956.

dishonour, are offered no earthly reward, but are promised the strength that works through weakness, and the joy that transforms pain. This is the good news that Paul proclaims, and of such a gospel he has indeed no need to feel ashamed.[35]

---

35 We have made no reference to the Pastoral Epistles in this chapter, because they are written in a distinct style of their own, and address a very different situation from that reflected in the rest of the Pauline epistles, and may therefore properly be attributed to a later writer. They contain occasional references to the death of Christ, largely couched in traditional language. He is described as the mediator between God and man, who gave himself as a ransom (*antilutron*) for (*huper*) all (1 Tim. 2.5f.). He gave himself for (*huper*) us, in order to ransom (*lutroō*) us from all wickedness and purify his own people for himself (Tit. 2.14). Some passages which sound like credal summaries omit any reference to Christ's death: 1 Tim. 1.15; 3.16. Elsewhere we have passing references to it: Jesus made the good confession in his testimony before Pontius Pilate (1 Tim. 6.13); he destroyed the power of death (2 Tim. 1.10). Some passages sound very much like fragments of Paul's teaching: in 2 Tim. 2.8 we have an odd summary of Paul's gospel, 'Remember Jesus Christ, risen from the dead, descended from David' (cf. Rom. 1.3f.), and a few verses later a quotation of a 'faithful saying' (v. 11): 'if we have died with him, we shall live with him' (cf. Rom. 6.8). Altogether, these references suggest that the author of the Pastorals was quoting familiar, traditional words that he had learned from Paul.

CHAPTER THREE

Mark

The gospel of Mark is almost certainly the earliest of our four canonical gospels, and we shall therefore consider it first.[1] The book is dominated by the death of Jesus to such an extent that it has been described as 'a passion narrative with a long introduction'.[2] Even in that long introduction there are hints of coming rejection,[3] while from Caesarea Philippi onwards, there are constant reminders of the way in which the story must end. Three times the passion predictions toll their knell; Jesus goes up to Jerusalem to die, and die he must. The story is repeated by the other evangelists, but because they add so much other material – accounts of Jesus' miracles, and of his teaching – the impact that they make on us is less intense. Read Mark's gospel at a sitting (as it was perhaps originally intended to be read), and you will see how quickly events move to a climax, how inevitably the cross casts its shadow over the whole story.

Why does this theme dominate the gospel in this way? The simplest answer is because the death of Jesus was important; because, as Paul says in 1 Corinthians, it is the heart of the gospel.[4] So, when Mark came to write the gospel in narrative form, he concentrated on this, rather than on the teaching and miracles. But we have already seen that when Paul reminded the Corinthians that he had preached 'Christ crucified' to them, it was probably because they were having problems with accepting the scandal of the cross. The death of Jesus – and in particular his crucifixion – caused problems

---

1 Scholars continue to debate the question of the order in which the gospels were written, but we believe that this is the most likely solution.
2 The phrase goes back to Martin Kähler, *The So-called Historical Jesus and the Historic, Biblical Christ*, 1892, Philadelphia, E. Tr. 1964, p. 80n: Kähler in fact used the phrase of *all* the gospels, though he referred chiefly to Mark.
3 E.g. 2.20, 3.6, 19.
4 1 Cor. 1.13, 17f., 23f., 2.2.

for the Corinthians: may it perhaps have caused problems in the community for whom Mark was writing? How could God's Messiah have been put to death on a cross? It just did not make sense! Perhaps we should see Mark's gospel primarily as a piece of Christian apologetic, explaining how it was that the Messiah had been put to death in this ignominious way. This would explain why Mark emphasizes the inevitability of the death of Christ and explains that he died in accordance with the scriptures: the death of the Messiah *did* make sense! So Mark describes how Jesus spelt out clearly and plainly to his disciples what was going to happen to him in Jerusalem. It was all written in scripture: it was part of the purpose of God. If only one has eyes to see – and makes use of them – it should be clear that it was in fact necessary for Jesus to die. It is difficult to believe that Jesus in fact spoke about his death with such clarity, for the disciples seem to have been unprepared for what happened, but as Christians looked back on the story, everything fell into place. Mark's gospel, in other words, is a bold apology for the scandal of the cross, written to help those who were unable to comprehend how God allowed his Messiah to be put to death.

Some commentators have suggested a very different explanation for Mark's emphasis on the cross, arguing that those for whom he was writing were not so much perplexed by the death of Jesus as offended by it. Like the Corinthians, they just did not want to know about a crucified Lord. Their Lord was risen, victorious – and the fact that victory came through apparent defeat was brushed aside as unpalatable. So, it is suggested, Mark wrote his gospel, not to explain the scandal of the cross, but to remind his readers that it was central to their faith,[5] and this is why he has a great deal to say about the death of Jesus and very little about the resurrection. Whichever explanation is correct, we can see that the cross presented Mark and his readers with a problem – a problem which he faces boldly.

One of the intriguing things about Mark's story is the way in which he links the death of Jesus with the suffering of others, both before him and after him. He links it first of all with the suffering of the one who goes immediately before

---

5 This view was argued by T. J. Weeden, *Mark: Traditions in Conflict*, Philadelphia 1971, though unfortunately he linked it with his theory that Mark was opposing a 'divine man' christology, set out in the miracle stories.

him and announces his coming, namely John the Baptist. The very first hint of the coming death of Jesus occurs in 1.14, where we are told that Jesus came into Galilee after the arrest of John. It is a somewhat obscure hint, and we may well miss it altogether, but when we have read the rest of the story we shall see its significance, for the verb which Mark uses for the arrest of John is *paradidōmi*, a word with which we are already familiar, since it is used by Paul when he speaks of Christ being given up for our sakes.[6] Mark uses the same verb later in the gospel when he speaks of Jesus being handed over into the power of evil men;[7] it is also the verb he uses of Judas handing over — i.e., betraying — Jesus.[8] Thus anyone who was familiar with the rest of the story which Mark has to tell would find this word ringing a bell. The first time round, you might miss its significance, but once you know what is going to happen later in the story, you inevitably make a link between what happens to John and what happens to Jesus. John, the forerunner of Jesus, who prepares the way before him, has been handed over into the power of Herod; and that means that his fate is sealed. In chapter 6, Mark tells us the sequel. Now this account of John the Baptist's death is very unusual, in that it is the only passage in Mark where attention is focused on someone other than Jesus himself; even the account of John's preaching in chapter 1 is no exception, since John's preaching is in fact all about the one who follows him, namely Jesus.[9] Yet here in chapter 6 we have this lurid and detailed account of the events which led to John's beheading. Why does Mark apparently desert the story about Jesus at this point to tell us about John? He has told us nothing else about him — nothing about his birth, as in Luke, nor even about the message he sent to Jesus from prison, about which we read in Matthew and Luke. The answer is surely that this story, too, is in fact no exception to the truth that Mark's attention is focused throughout his gospel on the figure of Jesus. If he pauses to tell us about how John died, it is only because in his death, as in his preaching, John is the forerunner of Jesus himself: John has been handed over into the power of men — as Jesus himself will be; he has been put to death — as Jesus

---

6 Rom. 4.25; Gal. 2.20.
7 9.31; 10.33. Cf. 15.1, 15.
8 3.19; 14.10f., 18, 21, 42, 44.
9 Contrast Matthew and Luke, who include additional teaching by John: Matt. 3.7–10; Luke 3.7–14.

will be. And though John and Jesus die in very different ways, there is an interesting parallel between the two stories in that a reluctant political ruler (Herod) is persuaded for the sake of expediency to put John to death, just as later a reluctant political ruler (Pilate) will be persuaded to crucify Jesus for the sake of expediency. Only the ending of the stories is different: in Mark 6, John's disciples come and bury him, and though there are rumours that he has been raised from the dead and has returned in the person of Jesus, such rumours are obviously false.

Just in case we do not grasp the significance of what has happened to John, Mark tells us about a conversation between Jesus and three of the disciples on the way down from the Mount of Transfiguration (9.9–13). On the mountain, Jesus has been seen talking with Elijah and Moses – appropriate enough companions, since each of them had experienced a theophany on a mountain. Another link between Jesus and these two figures is that, like him, each of them had experienced persecution: perhaps Mark saw them as in a sense sharing in advance in his sufferings.[10] As they descend from the mountain, the disciples remind Jesus about the tradition that Elijah is to return before the End. Jesus agrees that Elijah was indeed to come in order to prepare everything, but adds that in fact he has already come, and 'they have done whatever they wanted to him, even as it is written of him'. Commentators have never been able to discover a passage where Elijah's sufferings are foretold, but the significant point is that the returning Elijah is here clearly identified with John; he is the one who comes before the End, to prepare the way of the Lord. Elijah has already come – and look what has happened to him! If they do that to the messenger, what will they do to the Lord himself? Mark tells us that Jesus immediately links the fate of Elijah (alias John) with his own: 'How is it written of the Son of man, that he must suffer many things and be rejected?' The fate of Jesus and John are intertwined.

So when Mark describes how Jesus comes to the temple in Jerusalem and is challenged about the source of his authority, it should be no surprise that he responds with a counter-question to the Jewish authorities about the authority of John: was John's authority from heaven or from men? Those to whom the question is put dither, wondering how to answer it, but readers of the gospel are in no doubt

10 Cf. Heb. 11.26.

about the true answer: the authority of John was clearly from God. But why should Jesus put such a question? Because, of course, John is the predecessor of Jesus; if his authority had been accepted, so, too, would the authority of Jesus. But it was not. So what will happen to Jesus? If the one who prepared the way for him was rejected, the outcome is inevitable.

John the Baptist's function in Mark's gospel is to serve as the witness to Jesus, and he witnesses to him, not only in his preaching – in his proclamation of the one who follows him – but in his death, which seals the fate of Jesus himself. Just as scripture is seen as pointing forward to Jesus – to who he is and to the death he must die – so, too, does John the Baptist. The final irony comes in the story of the crucifixion itself, where the bystanders imagine that Jesus is calling on Elijah for aid. Why Elijah might be expected to come to rescue him we do not know: what we *do* know is that 'Elijah' *cannot* come, because he, too, has been put to death.

But Jesus' death is linked also with the fate of those who follow after him, and one of the remarkable features of Mark's story is the way in which it underlines the link between the death of Christ and the cost of discipleship. The early chapters of Mark do little to prepare us for this theme: there Jesus proclaims the Kingdom of God; he brings healing and forgiveness, new life and wholeness; the appropriate images would seem to be those of feasting (2.19) and of harvest (4.8). Is not this the time for rejoicing? But suddenly Jesus begins to talk about the death of the Son of man – and whatever the meaning of this strange term, Mark clearly supposes it to refer to Jesus. But does it include others beside Jesus? Does it perhaps refer to a community rather than an individual,[11] or was it perhaps (as has been argued recently) an Aramaic idiom meaning 'a man such as I am'?[12] Fortunately we do not have to come to a decision on this very complicated question here, but it is important to notice that whatever the original meaning of this phrase may have been, the sayings about the suffering, death and vindication of the Son of man clearly refer to Jesus, and yet just as clearly are relevant to the behaviour of his disciples. It has

11 T. W. Manson, *The Teaching of Jesus*, 2nd. edn. Cambridge 1935, pp. 211–36; M. D. Hooker, *The Son of Man in Mark*, London 1967, pp. 178–98.
12 E.g. G. Vermes, *Jesus the Jew*, London, 1973; M. Casey, *Son of Man*, London, 1979; B. Lindars, *Jesus, Son of Man*, London 1983.

been pointed out many times that each of the so-called 'passion predictions' is immediately followed by a scene in which we see what it means to be a disciple of one who is handed over into the power of men, who is rejected, who suffers and is put to death on a cross. I say 'so-called passion predictions' because in fact the predictions are of passion followed by vindication, of death followed by resurrection. Jesus accepts the inevitability of suffering, but he has total confidence that God's purpose cannot fail. Three times, according to Mark, he affirms that the way ahead includes both death and resurrection, and three times Mark shows us what these predictions mean for Jesus' disciples by following each one with a scene which spells out for them the significance of following a Master who is prepared to be crucified. The first, in 8.31, is followed by Jesus' challenge to the crowds: summoning the people, he begins, 'if anyone wishes to come after me . . . .' We can imagine the crowd listening with bated breath; we can imagine those listening to Mark's story for the first time, wondering what challenge to great and noble action was to follow. Jesus' demand continues: 'let him deny himself, and take up his cross, and follow me'. What sort of invitation is this? If you wish to be a disciple of Jesus you must deny yourself – you must have no thought for your own concerns and interests – and take up a cross! In other words, those who follow Jesus must embrace that cruel and shameful death which anyone in his right mind[13] would do anything to avoid! Imagine the impact on those who, unlike us, had not grown familiar

---

13 'His' seems the correct adjective here, since crucifixion was used almost exclusively as a punishment for men: I have been able to discover only two or three possible references to women being crucified, none of them unambiguous. This is hardly surprising, since women were unlikely to become armed rebels, though crucifixion might perhaps have been used as a punishment for female slaves. No doubt the humiliation involved in crucifixion seemed peculiarly appropriate for men who were being stripped of all pretence to power. None of the discussions of crucifixion that I have consulted raises the question as to whether it was confined to men or what equivalent punishment was used for female slaves. If the image is an inherently masculine one, this raises interesting questions regarding Jesus' challenge to discipleship. Was it addressed only to men? If so, was this because only men could be disciples? Or was it because men – rather than women – found the attitude which Jesus demanded so difficult? Jesus' sayings about discipleship sound paradoxical in a society where *men* seek positions of honour and regard those who serve as inferior: women might well have found them reassuring! One of the interesting features of Mark's gospel is that women – who are not

with these words; imagine the effect on those for whom crucifixion was no metaphor, but a real possibility. Those who tried to save their lives would lose them, while those who gave them up for the sake of Jesus would be saved. But if they were ashamed of Jesus and his absurd demands – ashamed of the one who had died in this shameful manner – then the Son of man would be ashamed of them, when he came in glory. Jesus himself loses his life, and is saved by God; he accepts shame, and receives glory; and he expects nothing less from his followers.

If the first thing we learn about Jesus' death was that it is now understood to have been inevitable, then the second is that it must be shared by others. Those who wish to be his disciples must live as he lived – and that means they must be prepared to die as he died. They must be willing to share his pain, his shame, his weakness, his death. His death is not seen as a substitute for theirs, but rather as a pattern. This call was taken seriously by many in the early Church. Ignatius of Antioch, for example, facing the prospect of martyrdom, describes himself as 'an imitator of the passion of my God', and says that his own death will be a 'sacrifice of God' and a 'ransom' for other Christians.[14]

The second prediction of what lies ahead in Jerusalem comes in 9.31. Again Jesus speaks of his coming death and resurrection. Mark tells us that the disciples did not understand and were afraid to ask. They certainly had not understood the first time, at Caesarea Philippi; hence Peter's blundering comment. This time they demonstrate their incomprehension by arguing, as they go along, about which of them is the greatest. It is difficult to think of a less appropriate subject for them to be discussing: here is Jesus talking about his coming death, and they argue about their own greatness! Jesus' rebuke begins like his earlier call, and it is equally paradoxical: 'If anyone wishes to be first,' he says, 'he must be last of all, and servant of all.' The disciples have failed to grasp that greatness comes through service. And what does service involve? For Jesus, at least, it means death, as we learn in the famous saying of 10.45: the Son of man came not to be served but to serve, and to give his life a

---

specifically called to *be* disciples – are those who prove to be real disciples by showing faith and offering service. See 1.31; 5.25–34; 7.25–9; 12.41–4; 14.3–9; 15.40f., 47; 16.1f.

14 *Romans* 6.3; 4.2; *Ephesians* 21.1; *Polycarp* 2.3; 6.1; *Smyrnaeans* 10.2.

ransom for many. This saying is given in response to another argument among the disciples. Once again, in 10.33, Jesus has spoken about his coming suffering, death and resurrection, and once again the disciples have shown their complete inability to grasp what he is saying, for James and John have come to Jesus requesting the places of honour, at his right and left hand, when he enters his glory. For us, Mark's story is full of irony, since we know what the disciples have failed to grasp, that Jesus will enter his glory through his death on the cross, and that James and John are therefore asking to die with him. In fact, it will be two thieves who occupy those places, for though James and John declare their readiness to share Jesus' baptism and drink his cup, they are not yet ready to do so.

By his placing of the material, Mark has emphasized the link between the sufferings of Jesus and the demands he makes of his disciples, so that we are left in no doubt that following Jesus involves both danger and dishonour. Why does he emphasize the cost of discipleship in this way? The usual answer is that he was writing for a persecuted community – the traditional place of composition is of course Rome, and though the Church there was not the only Christian community to face persecution, we do know that some of the Christians there died martyrs' deaths. Perhaps they had not expected to face suffering and death: if so, it would have helped those who were enduring persecution to be reminded that this was part of what being a disciple of Jesus meant. Perhaps they did not know these sayings of Jesus, and had not realized where their loyalty to him might bring them. Perhaps they had responded to the good news that the Kingdom of God was here, and thought that this was the end of the matter. Perhaps, like Peter, James and John, they had thought of discipleship in terms of honour and privilege, and were shocked by the demands their loyalty to Jesus made on them. If so, then Mark's emphasis on the necessity of suffering for both Jesus and his followers has a very practical purpose. Or perhaps the community was not yet facing persecution, but like the Corinthian Church saw their Christian discipleship in terms of gain and advantage. If so, they would certainly need to be reminded that Jesus had warned his disciples that they must share his baptism and drink his cup, and that following a crucified Lord was likely to involve them, too, in shame and suffering.

Mark emphasizes the necessity for suffering – both Jesus' own, and that of his disciples, but he says almost nothing about its meaning. It is necessary for Jesus to die; it is written that he must suffer. But *why*? A couple of years ago, I watched a television programme about Ireland; it was not, in fact a very good programme, but its theme was memorable, for it was about a father whose son had been brutally murdered by the IRA, and who set off for Ireland with two questions in his mind. The first was the question about how his son had died; he wanted to see the place for himself and establish the facts; the second was the inevitable question as to *why* he had died; he was looking, he said, for some kind of meaning in it all, an explanation which would help him to feel that his son had not died for nothing.

A lot of Mark's story looks at the death of Jesus with the first of those questions in mind – how did Jesus die? – but occasionally we are confronted with the second – *why* did he die? One passage which gives an answer to this is 10.45, which we referred to a moment ago: the death of Jesus is part of his service for others; he dies as a ransom for many. This passage is often explained as a reference to Isaiah 53, where the Servant's death is interpreted as a sin-offering for many. That passage has played a very large part in Christian understanding of Jesus' death, and we naturally expect the evangelists to have used it also. In fact, however, the language of Mark 10.45 is quite different from that of Isaiah 53.[15] The background is, I suggest, much broader than Isaiah 53: the word translated 'ransom', *lutron*, means something which is paid in order to get something back, while the verb *lutroō* is used in the Old Testament of God's redemption of his people, first of all from slavery in Egypt, and later of his bringing them back from Exile in Babylon – in other words, of God's basic activity in saving his people and establishing them *as* his people. In Mark 10.45 we are told that Jesus dies as a ransom for many. Now that word 'many' can mislead us in two ways. First of all, we tend to use it in an exclusive way – we assume, that is, that it means 'some' – a lot, that is, but not everyone; in Jewish writings, however, the word was normally used in an inclusive way, as a parallel to 'all'. And linked to this is the other difference in meaning – namely, that when we use the word 'many'

---

15 For a fuller discussion of this, see M. D. Hooker, *Jesus and the Servant*, London 1959, pp. 74–9, *The Son of Man in Mark*, London 1967, pp. 140–7, and C. K. Barrett, 'The background of Mark 10.45' in *New Testament Essays: Studies in Memory of Thomas Walter Manson*, ed. A. J. B. Higgins, Manchester 1959, pp. 1–18.

today we tend to think of a lot of individuals, whereas for the Jews the word probably refers to a community; we find it used at Qumran, for example, to refer to the community there. What these words in Mark 10.45 affirm, then, is not that Jesus' death saves certain individuals, but that it is the saving action by which God establishes his new people.

If Jesus' death is a saving act parallel to the Exodus and the Return, from what does he save his people? Surprisingly, Mark never spells this out, but there are hints throughout his gospel. One is found in the dramatic imagery of 3.23–7, where Jesus' mission is seen as the defeat of Satan and the rescue of men and women from his power. Others come in the references to forgiveness. The baptism of John which prepared men and women for Jesus' coming was 'for the forgiveness of sins' (1.4), and forgiveness is part of the salvation that Jesus himself offers to those who respond to his message (2.1–12); those who *refuse* to respond are hard of heart and under divine judgement (11.12–20; 12.9; 13.1–36; 8.38; 14.62). At the end, his disciples are offered forgiveness in spite of their failure to stand by him (16.7): the new company created by Jesus' death and resurrection is thus the forgiven community.

* * *

Mark's story follows Jesus and his disciples from Galilee, through the regions of Judea and Transjordan, to Jerusalem. When we come to the passion narrative, we shall discover Mark stressing that Jesus dies as 'King of the Jews', and already as he approaches Jerusalem, the idea begins to surface. Leaving Jericho, he is hailed as Son of David (10.47f.), and he enters the royal city, riding like a king and welcomed as king by the plaudits of the crowds. Having arrived in Jerusalem, his first action is to go to the temple, where he looks around at everything and withdraws. Next day, on the way to the temple, he inspects a fig-tree, discovers it to be barren, and pronounces a curse on it. In Jerusalem, he complains that the authorities have prevented the temple being what God intended, a house of prayer for all the nations: there is no fruit here, either, so he drives out the buyers and sellers of animals and overthrows the money tables. Jesus' violent action in the temple matches his violent words to the fig-tree – which is discovered, the next morning, to be dead – and it is clear from the way in which Mark has told these two stories that he intends us to see a link between them. The story of the fig-tree is an acted

parable of the fate of Israel, and Jesus' actions in the temple
are a symbol of its coming destruction and the cessation of
worship there altogether. Jesus' actions outrage the Jewish
religious leaders, who challenge his authority, and plot
together to destroy him; his protest thus leads directly to his
death. The charge brought against him by the Jewish
authorities is that he threatened to destroy the temple, but
the irony is that it is his death which makes the destruction
of Jerusalem and of the temple inevitable: Israel has finally
rejected her Messiah, and will in turn be rejected by God.

This theme comes to a climax in chapter 12, but of course
it runs right through the gospel, where scribes and Pharisees
continually object to what Jesus says and does. The fact that
their attitude is part of God's plan and that their hearts have
been hardened by him does not absolve them from guilt, any
more than it absolves Judas in 14.21, for divine predestina-
tion and human responsibility are held together in Mark.
The story is set out in an allegory in chapter 12: the owner
of a vineyard has sent his messengers to collect the fruit from
his vineyard, but they have been beaten and killed by the
tenants; finally he sends his only son, whereupon the tenants
plot together and kill him. What, asks Jesus, will the end of
the story be? He answers his own question: the vineyard
owner will come and destroy the tenants and hand the
vineyard over to others. The rejection of Jesus as Israel's
Messiah and of Israel as God's people are bound up
together: if the death of Jesus is inevitable, so, too, is the
destruction of Jerusalem and the holy temple. This is spelt
out in the so-called apocalyptic discourse in chapter 13 – but
notice that before judgement comes upon Israel, the disciples
will themselves have to endure suffering. It is no surprise to
find that the pattern of their suffering will echo that of Jesus:
they too will be delivered up to councils, made to stand
before governors; they will be beaten, brought to trial.
Because Jesus has been rejected, of course his followers will
be rejected, but the nation which rejects them is itself under
judgement and condemnation.

The passion narrative itself begins in 14.1: two days
before Passover, the priests and scribes combine forces to
plot how to take hold of Jesus. The strange thing is that
these opening verses suggest that Jesus was *not* taken and
killed during the Passover – in which case the Last Supper
was not a Passover meal. It is well-known that there is a
problem of dating with the Last Supper: the Synoptics
clearly understand it to be a Passover meal, while John (who

of course has a very different tradition about the Last Supper), tells us that Jesus died on the eve of Passover, at the very moment that the Passover lambs were being slain – a dating which agrees with a very much later statement in the Babylonian Talmud that Jesus was put to death on Passover Eve.[16] It is not my intention to enter the debate about the historical evidence: it used to be supposed that the Synoptics were right and that John had altered the date for theological reasons; with the realization that Mark was as much of a theologian in his own way as was John came the suggestion that it is John's dating which is correct. Some commentators have argued that different groups in Judaism celebrated Passover on different days, and that both traditions are therefore correct: Jesus celebrated Passover on the Thursday night, as Mark records, but the official celebration fell one day later, as John tells us.[17] I myself think that this last explanation is too ingenious, and I am inclined to believe that John has given us the correct dating. Mark's story raises all sorts of problems – not least, how the gathering of the Sanhedrin which led to the handing over of Jesus to the Roman authorities could have been held on Passover night; moreover, his account of what happened conflicts with the authorities' decision to do away with Jesus – but not during the festival. There is, in fact, nothing in Mark's account of the Last Supper itself to indicate that the meal was a Passover, and it is only the story of the preparation, in 14.12–16, that identifies it as such. It may be that Mark simply assumed that because it was Passover time, this last meal of Jesus with his disciples must have been a Passover. It may be that Jesus, suspecting that his arrest was imminent, deliberately 'echoed', by his symbolic words and actions, the Passover ritual which would take place on the following evening:[18] there would have been, of course, no Passover lamb, but there was bread and there was wine, and Jesus explains their meaning, just as the head of the family would explain other elements of the meal at Passover. But much more important – and much more interesting, too – than the historical problem is the theological interpretation which has been given to the tradition by our evangelists, for in their

16 B. T. Sanhedrin 43a.
17 A. Jaubert, *The Date of the Last Supper*, E. Tr., New York 1965.
18 Jesus' words in Luke 22.15f. imply that he will not eat the Passover, and taken on their own, out of context, are consistent with the Johannine dating, though Luke himself assumed that the Last Supper was a Passover.

very different ways, both Mark and John are expressing the same truth about Jesus' death – that it is the new Passover, through which God redeems his people. John believes that Jesus dies on the very day and at the very hour when the Passover lambs were slain: his sacrifice replaces the Passover lambs of Judaism. Mark knows that Jesus died at Passover time, and believes that the Last Supper must therefore have been a Passover meal, but the significance of that meal is centred on the death of Jesus: for Mark, too, Jesus' death replaces that of the Passover lambs.

Jesus' actions at the Last Supper (14.22–5) are accompanied by two brief sayings: giving the disciples the bread, he says 'This is my body'. Unlike the Pauline version of the saying, Mark's version does not contain the words 'for you', nor the command to repeat the action in Jesus' memory. On their own, the words could be an expression of Jesus' fellowship with his disciples, or a handing over of responsibility – a commission to carry on his work – but in the context of the Last Supper, Mark probably understands them as an explanation of the significance of Jesus' death. The words over the cup are clearer, even though they raise a host of problems: 'This is my blood of the covenant, shed for many'. The reference to the covenant takes us back to the covenant made between God and his people on Sinai, which established them as his people. The covenant made through Jesus' death is made on behalf of 'many', and we have already seen that the word 'many' refers to a community, rather than to a lot of individuals. Jesus' blood seals a new covenant, and in doing so establishes a new community. It is significant that both of the sayings in Mark which refer to the purpose of Christ's death – both 10.45 and the saying here, in 14.24 – echo language used in the Old Testament about God's election of Israel, and look back to the Exodus and to Sinai: through Christ's death a new people of God is created. The saying over the cup leads into another: Jesus declares that he will not drink wine again until the day when he drinks it new in the Kingdom of God. Notice the confidence of this saying: the Kingdom of God is coming – moreover, Jesus himself will share in its joys! Immediately after a saying about his death, therefore, we have another which looks forward to his vindication: Jesus expects to die – but he is confident that God will restore him. Possibly the saying implies more, for it could be understood as indicating that the death of Jesus is the means by which the Kingdom of God will arrive.

But in looking at the Last Supper we have missed out one important story which Mark places just before it, inbetween the statement that the chief priests and scribes were plotting how to take Jesus by stealth and the resolution of their problem with Judas' promise to betray him. In 14.3–9 he describes the anointing of Jesus by a woman, who bursts into the supper party where Jesus is being entertained and pours aromatic oil over his head. Her extravagant action in breaking the jar and pouring out a vast amount of expensive ointment symbolizes the anointing of Jesus' body for burial. In fact, of course, the dead body of Jesus was never anointed, since the women who came to anoint his body were prevented by the resurrection. The woman's action thus points forward not only to Jesus' death but to his resurrection, and proclaims them both, and this is why her action will be remembered wherever the gospel is preached. But the story suggests something else. The woman does not anoint Jesus' feet, which would have been a courtesy customarily rendered to a traveller, but his head. Why? Two days later, Jesus is asked by the high priest whether or not he is God's Messiah and his Son. As high priest, it was Caiaphas' responsibility to recognize the Messiah, to anoint him as king, and to proclaim him to Israel, but this he fails to do. The truth is affirmed by Jesus himself when he replies 'I am' to Caiaphas' questions, but the anointing is carried out by a woman, while the proclamation of Jesus to Israel as king will be made by Pilate and the declaration that he is the Son of God by Jesus' executioner. The irony is clear: the very notion that a woman could anoint Israel's king is absurd, for a woman was the very last person to have the authority to do any such thing! Moreover, her action points forward to his burial, because it is by his death that Jesus is recognized as king of Israel, and through his death and resurrection that he is acknowledged as Son of God. The whole story is absurd – a woman and two Gentiles have usurped the high priest's powers! – and yet entirely appropriate in a gospel which is about greatness expressed in service, and about the last who come first. A Messiah who is proclaimed king through a shameful death can certainly accept anointing from the hands of a humble woman.

Now the truth that Jesus is proclaimed king *on the cross* is one for which Mark has already prepared us, and is perhaps the key to his understanding of the death of Jesus. When at Caesarea Philippi the disciples acknowledge him as Messiah, the disciples are told to say nothing, and Jesus immediately switches the conversation and begins to teach them that the Son of man must suffer and die. His messiahship can be understood only by those who grasp the truth that it will be proclaimed through his death. At the Transfiguration, Jesus is seen in glory and revealed as Son of God to three disciples, but they are told to say nothing until the Son of man is raised; the glory is a glimpse of who Jesus is, but it can be revealed to men and women only through his death and resurrection. The paradoxical truth which Jesus sets before would-be disciples that greatness comes through service, and glory through shame, is true for them only because it is true first and foremost for Jesus himself. Throughout Mark's gospel the identity of Jesus has been concealed: but when we come to the story of the crucifixion, it is announced for everyone to hear. From the moment that the high priest asks 'Are you the Messiah?' and Jesus replies 'I am', the truth is proclaimed; the high priest asked the right question, even though he refused to accept the reply. When Jesus is brought before the Roman prefect, Pilate asks a similar question – not, as we might expect, 'Do you *claim* to be the king of the Jews?' but '*Are* you the king of the Jews?' Jesus replies *su legeis* – 'You have said it', or perhaps 'The words are yours'. Like the high priest, Pilate has unwittingly declared the truth. Moreover, in his conversation with the Jews, Pilate continues referring to Jesus as 'the king of the Jews', as though he believed the claim to be true (15.9,12). The Roman soldiers mock him as 'king of the Jews' (v. 18); the inscription on the cross reads 'the king of the Jews' (v. 26); and finally the chief priests and scribes mock him as 'the Messiah, the king of Israel' (v. 32). Of course, none of these people believe that he is what they call him. The irony of Mark's story is that Jesus is revealed as the Messiah on the cross, and no one has eyes of faith to recognize him; there is, of course, one exception to that, whom we must look at in a moment.

Following on the Last Supper, we have the story of Gethsemane – in many ways the most moving and difficult in the whole of the gospel. This is one of the few events in the life of Jesus that is referred to outside the gospels, for we find a reference to it in Heb. 5.7–8. There is no reason to question it historically, for the story of Jesus' anguish in the garden rings true; the difficulty with it is that it conflicts to some extent with the picture which Mark has been giving us. From at least Caesarea Philippi onwards Jesus has known what the end of the story must be; we have observed the note of total certainty in the predictions of his coming suffering and vindication. But if Jesus has accepted death as God's will, believes it to be written in scripture, and sees it as the cup which he must drink, why the hesitation now? Why does he pray at this late stage for the cup to be removed? If the story were about anyone else, we would think it sounded like a failure of nerve at the eleventh hour. But if it is not that, why does he waver now? How *can* the cup be taken away? If this is indeed authentic tradition, does it not suggest that Mark has emphasized the certainty with which Jesus spoke of his future suffering? Is it not more likely that Jesus spoke of the *probability* of rejection and of his willingness to drink the cup *if it were necessary*, and that he hoped to the end that men and women would respond to his message? We have seen already that it is difficult to believe that he foretold his future sufferings with the clarity and detail suggested by Mark – much more likely that he expressed his trust in God and his confidence that God would vindicate him whatever happened. It would be natural enough for men and women looking back after the resurrection to think 'So that's what he meant!' and interpret his words as clear prophecies of what was going to happen. But these are historical problems, and we are concerned primarily with the way in which Mark tells his story, and what he wishes us to hear. Notice how in this story Peter, James and John are given an opportunity to share in Jesus' anguish and to help him. Immediately before, Peter has boasted that he will never desert Jesus (14.26–31); earlier, James and John had boasted that they could drink Jesus' cup and share his baptism. Now they are given the opportunity to make good those boasts – and they fail miserably; in contrast, Jesus is faithful and obedient, and though he prays that the cup may be taken from him, he is nevertheless willing to drink it. 'Abba', he prays, using the Aramaic term for 'Father' – and the word sums up his willingness to obey, whatever it may cost.

The story of the arrest (14.45–52) underlines again the theme of fulfilment of scripture in Jesus' words 'Let the scriptures be fulfilled'. Which scriptures we are not told: echoes of the Old Testament scriptures occur throughout the story, but the most influential seems to be Psalm 22, the psalm of the righteous sufferer, which is quoted in 15.24, 29 and 34. By showing how the death of Jesus corresponds with scripture, Mark uses the Old Testament to explain the scandal of the cross. The arrest is made by a rabble 'sent by the chief priests, scribes and elders', guided to the spot by Judas. Mark offers no explanation for Judas' treachery – though he mentions that he was promised money in 14.11; like the death of Jesus itself, the act of betrayal is seen as part of what is written.[19]

The account of the interrogation by Caiaphas (14.55–65) emphasizes the innocence of Jesus: the witnesses against him were false – and even so they could not agree! The charge that Jesus has threatened to destroy the temple is absurd, though he has of course spoken (in private, to four disciples) about its coming destruction, and about the judgement which is going to come on Israel. Once again, we see how the fate of Jesus is tied up with the fate of the nation: if the Jewish authorities condemn Jesus to death, it will in fact be they who are bringing down destruction upon themselves and upon the temple. Jesus is finally condemned on a charge of blasphemy – though in fact he has not said anything which could have been regarded as blasphemous according to the rules. The high priest's verdict is as false as the evidence given by the witnesses – indeed the whole proceedings are illegal according to Jewish law. Nevertheless, the truth about Jesus is unwittingly proclaimed: for he is the Messiah, the Son of the Blessed one; the temple will indeed be destroyed and a new one (the Christian community) will be built in its place.

With this story of the so-called 'trial', Mark interweaves another, which relates how Peter, in the courtyard below, is challenged as one of Jesus' followers, and denies all knowledge of him. With supreme irony Mark depicts Jesus finally acknowledging openly that he is the Messiah, and as a result condemned to death, at the very moment that Peter, who has sworn to be loyal to him to death, denies that he is his disciple. When the Son of man comes with the clouds of heaven, will he be ashamed of one who has been ashamed of him?[20]

The innocence of Jesus is stressed again in the account of the trial before Pilate. Jesus is 'handed over' to Pilate by the Jerusalem authorities, who bring many accusations against him, but Pilate realizes very well that there is no substance in the charges they have made against him. He attempts to release Jesus, since it was customary, says Mark, for him to release a prisoner (chosen by the people!) at the festival:

---

19 14.21. V.18 echoes Ps. 41.9, which is quoted in John 13.18.
20 14.62; 8.38.

there is no evidence outside the gospels for this unlikely custom. The incident, improbable as it is, serves to emphasize the guilt of the Jews: they demand the release of the guilty Barabbas and urge Pilate to crucify Jesus. Pilate, though he declares Jesus to have done nothing wrong, succumbs, and 'hands over' Jesus to be crucified.

Now the kingship of Jesus comes to the fore: presumably the Jews are to be understood as having accused Jesus of claiming to be 'king of the Jews'. Three times Pilate refers to Jesus as 'the king of the Jews' (vv. 2–12); and the 'charge' nailed above his head reads 'the king of the Jews' (v. 26).

The charges brought against Jesus by the false witnesses and by the Jewish leaders are picked up by the passers-by, who mock Jesus as he hangs on the cross and address him as the one who would destroy the temple and rebuild it in three days. 'He saved others,' say the chief priests and scribes, 'but he cannot save himself.' To Mark's readers, who know the truth about Jesus, the irony in their taunts is clear: though they do not realize it, it is precisely because he does not save himself that he is able to save others. 'Let the Messiah, the king of Israel come down from the cross, that we may see and believe.' In fact it is because he does not come down from the cross that men and women do come to see and believe that he is 'the Messiah, the king of Israel.' The helpless crucified figure on the cross confirms the truth of the inscription, nailed above his head in mockery, which proclaims him as king.

The darkness which covers the land at the sixth hour is reminiscent of Amos 8.9, where it is a sign of judgement on the Day of the Lord. Jesus' cry in v. 34 comes from Psalm 22, which describes the sufferings of the righteous. Once again Jesus addresses God in Aramaic – 'Eloi, Eloi – my God, my God, why have you forsaken me?' It is typical of Mark's story that the bystanders do not comprehend him and think that he is calling on Elijah to deliver him: they have no understanding of the true significance of what is taking place. Jesus' words are a cry of dereliction, and though countless commentators have suggested that Mark means us to understand that Jesus was thinking of the whole psalm and that they are in fact a cry of hope, there is no indication of this in the text. The suggestion is due to the pious belief that Jesus' last words could not have been a cry of despair: but Mark tells us that they were, and I believe that he intended us to grapple with the story as he tells it. There is darkness over the whole land, from the sixth to the

ninth hour – a darkness so great that it engulfs Jesus himself.
He feels himself to be abandoned by God: this is surely
Mark's equivalent of Paul's statement that Christ was made
a curse and that he was made sin.[21] He drinks the cup of
suffering to the full; he experiences the ultimate despair. But
we, the readers of the Gospel, know that the darkness
symbolizes God's judgement on Israel, not on Jesus.

When Jesus dies, the curtain of the temple is torn from top
to bottom. After all that has been said about the temple,
Mark certainly intends us to see this as symbolic. But what
does it signify? Is this, too, a sign of God's judgement on his
people? Does it point forward to the future destruction of
the temple? Is it a sign that the Jewish sacrificial system has
come to an end? Or is it positive rather than negative – does
it indicate that the old barriers have been broken down, and
that there is now a new access to God? But of course, these
two ideas belong together: Israel is condemned, but a new
community is born. At the very moment that the curtain is
torn, a Gentile breaks through the barrier, as Jesus'
executioner, the Roman centurion, seeing how he dies,
declares: 'truly this man was [the] Son of God'. It sounds an
unlikely confession – though to a Roman centurion, 'son of
God' would perhaps have meant little more than 'a righteous
man'.[22] For Mark, however, his words are the appropriate
response to the death of Jesus. This is the moment of
supreme irony: the Jews failed to recognize Jesus as their
Messiah; even the disciples found it hard to grasp who he
was; but an outsider, a Gentile, who knew nothing at all
about Jesus except the manner of his death, confesses Jesus
as Son of God! It is in dying that Jesus is recognized as
Messiah and acknowledged as God's Son.

Mark's story concludes with a brief account of how the
women came to the tomb and found it empty, apart from a
young man in white who gave them a message to take to 'the
disciples and Peter'. Who, we wonder, are these disciples?
Did they not all in effect renounce their discipleship when
they deserted him in the garden? And though Peter belatedly
returned and followed Jesus as far as the high priest's
courtyard, he there denied three times any knowledge of

21 Gal. 3.13; 2 Cor. 5.21.
22 There is no article before 'Son of God' in Greek, which means that the
phrase is ambiguous: one can translate 'a son of God' or 'the Son of God'.
Words which, in the mouth of a centurion, could have only the lesser
meaning, are interpreted by Mark at a higher level and as an expression of
the truth about Jesus.

Jesus – let alone that he was a disciple! We remember Jesus' demand that the true disciple must deny[23] him or her *self*, and his warning that those who are ashamed of Jesus will find that the Son of man will be ashamed of them when he comes in glory.[24] But now Peter is singled out and included in the group who are commanded to follow to Galilee: it is not yet too late for them to become disciples once more. The message is thus not simply a command, but an assurance that the death and resurrection of Jesus bring forgiveness and the opportunity to begin again: through his death, a new community has indeed been created.

The message to the disciples echoes Jesus' words in 14.28. Everything he had told them in the upper room has been fulfilled: one of his disciples betrayed him, another denied him; all of them lost faith; the shepherd was struck and the sheep were scattered. Now his promise to go before them into Galilee is also fulfilled. His message is a challenge to the disciples: 'the Risen Lord has gone before you into Galilee; follow him, and you will see him there'. We expect Mark to tell us how they obeyed and went to Galilee, but instead the narrative breaks off abruptly at 16.8: the women, we are told, 'went out and fled from the tomb, overcome by trembling and terror, and they said nothing to anyone, for they were afraid.' These are Mark's last words: instead of giving us accounts of resurrection appearances, he leaves us in mid-air, wondering what happened next – though this is not always clear from our printed Bibles, since translators usually include the 'endings' to the gospel with which early editors of the text, dissatisfied with an apparently incomplete story, have rounded it off.[25] It has often been supposed that Mark's original ending has been lost, or that he never completed his manuscript; possibly the man who saw so clearly that being a disciple of Jesus could mean taking up the cross and following him to execution was called on to do just that. But I am inclined to believe that Mark ended his story at 16.8 deliberately.[26] The women flee in terror, overcome with fear at the mighty activity of God, and tell no one what has happened. We should not be surprised if Mark

---

23 The verb *aparneomai*, to deny, used in 8.34, is used also in 14.30f., 72.

24 8.38, 34.

25 The so-called 'longer ending' is usually printed as vv. 9–20. The 'shorter ending' has no verse enumeration.

26 M. D. Hooker, *The Gospel according to St Mark*, London 1991, pp. 391–4.

ends with a description of human fear and failure, since these have been the common reactions to Jesus throughout the story – and now the women are confronted with the most stupendous divine act of all: no wonder they are overcome with fear and fail to deliver the message! But we *are* perhaps surprised that he does not end with stories about the Risen Jesus: we expect reassurance that Jesus has indeed been raised, and that his body has not simply been stolen from the tomb. The other evangelists added accounts of meetings between Jesus and his disciples; why did Mark not do the same? He leaves us asking: 'Yes – but what happened next?'

And he leaves us to supply the answer! Mark's gospel concludes with a challenge to the disciples to set off to Galilee – to follow Jesus, once again, in the way of discipleship; if they obey – and only if they obey – they will see the Risen Lord. But is this message not a challenge also to Mark's readers? They, too, must follow Jesus on the way of discipleship if they want to see him. Had Mark ended with resurrection stories, we might have thought (as Christians have sometimes been tempted to think): 'so that's the end of the story; everything is now tidied up.' But for Mark, the resurrection of Jesus is only the beginning. He does not offer us – how could he? – cast-iron 'evidence' that Jesus has been raised from the dead, but confronts us instead with a challenge to believe and to follow.

The death of Jesus is the beginning of something new: it is the ransom which creates a new people, the means of establishing a new covenant, the event which signifies the destruction of the temple and the beginning of a new form of worship. But those who belong to this new community are those who are prepared to follow Jesus in the way of discipleship, who are not ashamed of him and of his call to take up the cross. The death and resurrection of Jesus do not absolve the disciple from the need to obey that call but reaffirm it. His death is not a substitute, but an exemplar. True disciples of Jesus will still be found, trudging along the road that leads to a cross, following their crucified and risen Lord.

CHAPTER FOUR
Matthew

The three synoptic gospels – Matthew, Mark and Luke – are so similar in outline and wording that it seems almost certain that there is some kind of literary relationship between them: although a few scholars argue for the priority of Matthew, the majority believe that this relationship is best explained by the supposition that Mark was the earliest of the three and was used by both Matthew and Luke. Certainly the way in which the three evangelists handle the death of Jesus supports this theory. In this chapter we assume that this explanation is the correct one.

Matthew repeats all the Markan predictions of the passion and resurrection, together with the 'ransom' saying of Mark 10.45 (Matt. 20.28); in addition, he has material relating to the passion that is not used by Mark. Nevertheless, the theme of Jesus' death does not dominate his gospel as it does Mark's. The reason is perhaps that Matthew's gospel, being much larger than Mark's, incorporates other material – e.g. long blocks of teaching – which means that our attention is not concentrated on the cross in the way that it is by Mark.

One surprising feature in Matthew is the fact that he does not quote any particular Old Testament text as having been fulfilled in the death of Jesus. This is surprising precisely because elsewhere Matthew does frequently spell out the way in which the Old Testament is fulfilled in the life and actions of Jesus. Though he emphasizes in the passion narrative (as does Mark) his belief that the scriptures are being fulfilled, occasionally adding to Mark's own statements to this effect (e.g. Matt. 26.54), and though there are frequent allusions there to Old Testament passages (some of which Mark does not make, e.g. Matt. 27.43, quoting Ps. 22.8), he nowhere says (as he often does in other contexts) that what happens to Jesus takes place in order that a particular passage of scripture might be fulfilled.[1] There is only one occasion in the passion narrative when he quotes a 'prophecy' and says that it has been fulfilled, and that is when he describes the purchase of the potter's field with the money paid to Judas (27.9f.). This failure to spell out how Jesus' death fulfils scripture is surprising to the modern reader, who wonders why Matthew, so fond of quoting scripture, does not quote what seems to us to be the obvious passage in Isaiah 53. The omission is even more amazing in view of the fact that Matthew certainly knew this passage, as is evidenced by the fact that he quotes Isa. 53.4 earlier in his gospel, at 8.17, and says that the prophet's words were fulfilled in the healing miracles: astonishing as it seems to us, Matthew apparently did not regard Isaiah 53 as the obvious passage to use with reference to Jesus' death. The passages which are most influential in his telling of the story of the passion are the psalms of lament, which describe the sufferings of the righteous who are persecuted by the wicked but who trust in God for final justification. This, as we shall see, accords with the way in which Matthew tells his story.

Yet if Matthew failed to use scripture in the way we expect, he did make his own contribution to the theme. Already in chapter 2 we have an ominous hint of the end of the story, when Herod attempts to kill Jesus. On this occasion it is the political ruler, King Herod, who sets out to remove a possible rival, and the religious leaders, the chief priests and scribes, who play an unintentional part in events by telling him where to find the child: at the end of the story, the roles will be reversed, and it will be the chief priests and scribes who engineer Jesus' death, the political ruler, Pilate, who reluctantly assists them.

Matthew's passion narrative opens in 26.1f. with an announcement by Jesus to his disciples telling them what is about to happen. In Mark's account, it is the evangelist who tells us that it was two days before the Passover, but in Matthew, it is Jesus himself who says: 'You know that in two days' time it will be the Passover, and the Son of man will be handed over to be crucified'. The change is significant: instead of Mark's simple reference to the date, Matthew reminds us that what is about to take place is all

---

1 The quotation of Ps. 22.19, given in the margin of some translations at 27.35, is found in late mss, and is generally thought to be an addition copied from John 19.24.

part of the divine plan, in which Jesus himself is a willing participant.

Matthew's description of the religious leaders' plot and of the anointing at Bethany are very similar to Mark's, though there are minor variations; in the latter story, Matthew singles out the fact that the perfume was 'very costly', and tells us that it could have been sold 'for a large sum', rather than for Mark's more precise figure of 'over three hundred denarii'. In the account of Judas' meeting with the chief priests which follows immediately afterwards we find other significant changes, for in Matthew Judas' motive is clearly avarice: 'What will you give me,' he asks, 'if I betray him to you?' Then (in words taken from Zech. 11.12) we are told that they paid him thirty pieces of silver. Matthew not only provides an explanation for Judas' behaviour, but presents us with an interesting contrast between the unknown woman and Judas. While she (in the eyes of the disciples)[2] squanders a vast sum of money in an attempt to express her devotion to Jesus, he betrays him for a mere thirty pieces of silver.[3]   The second story follows hard on the heels of the first, suggesting to us that it could have been Judas' disgust at Jesus' commendation of the woman's extravagant gesture which led him to betray him for money.

The account of the preparations for the Passover meal (26.17–19) is much shorter than Mark's, but the wording is very similar. The most interesting change comes in the message sent by Jesus to a Jerusalem householder (26.18), for instead of asking, as in Mark and Luke, 'where is the upper room where I may eat the Passover with my disciples?' he announces 'My time is near; I will keep the Passover in your house with my disciples'. The reference to 'my time' has a Johannine ring to it: Jesus is in control, and he does not need to ask for favours, but simply announces what he intends to do. In the next paragraph, similarly, Matthew's account is close to Mark's, but his final addition, in 26.25, indicates that Jesus is in command of events. Jesus has prophesied his betrayal, and the disciples have asked, in turn, 'Surely you don't mean me?' Now Judas uses exactly the same words, and the form of the question in Greek implies that he expects a negative answer! It is as though

---

2 The disciples here replace the unnamed critics in Mark's version: Matt. 26.8, cf. Mark 14.4.

3 If the 'pieces' were shekels, this would be equivalent to approximately 120 denarii.

Judas is a puppet, unaware of what he is doing: it is Jesus who informs him that he is his betrayer.

There may well be an echo of this idea later in Matthew's story, in 26.50, when Judas greets Jesus with a kiss in the garden. Judas addresses Jesus as 'Friend', using a word (*etairos*) which is found in the New Testament only in Matthew, always with a sense of reproach.[4] His next words are ambiguous: Is that what you are here for?' or, more probably, 'Do what you are here to do'. The latter fits in with 26.18: it is Jesus, not Judas, who gives the orders and who is in control of the situation.

Matthew's version of the Last Supper (26.26–9) follows Mark's closely, but he makes three small but important changes. To the words over the bread he adds the command 'eat', so shifting the emphasis from the simple sharing of the one loaf (the taking) to the actual eating of it. Secondly, in describing the cup he changes Mark's *epion* ('drank') to *piete* ('drink!') so that the statement that they all drank of it is replaced with yet another command, 'drink of it, all of you'. These changes no doubt reflect the way in which the Lord's Supper was being celebrated in the Matthaean community: attention was now focused on eating the bread and drinking the wine. And thirdly, he adds the words 'for the forgiveness of sins' to the saying about Jesus' blood. This introduces a new idea into the story, since Mark's account referred simply to the covenant between God and his people, a covenant which forged a new relationship between them rather than dealing with past sins. Matthew's is the only account of the Last Supper to make reference to the idea of forgiveness. One interesting fact is that the phrase 'for the forgiveness of sins' is used by Mark and Luke (but not by Matthew!) of John's baptism of repentance:[5] did Matthew deliberately transfer it from the baptism of John to the death of Jesus? Whatever the explanation, we have here one of the rare statements in the gospels that attempts to explain what the death of Jesus achieved.

Matthew's account of the prophecy of Peter's denial and the agony in the garden (26.30–46) are very close to Mark's, though he spells out more clearly than does Mark the three-fold prayer of Jesus in Gethsemane, so emphasizing the contrast between Peter's triple denial and Jesus' own steadfastness in the face of temptation. The words of Jesus'

4 Matt. 11.16; 20.13; 22.12.
5 Mark 1.4; Luke 3.3.

prayer echo a petition in the prayer he taught his disciples (6.10), strengthening Mark's picture of Jesus as totally obedient to God's will.

Matthew makes a significant addition to the story of the arrest (26.47–56) with Jesus' rebuke of the disciple who cut off the high priest's servant's ear. Jesus rejects the use of force: he could if he wished call on his Father for aid and be sent twelve legions of angels, but if he did, how would the scriptures be fulfilled? Once again, we see Jesus very much in command of the situation: what is about to happen could be avoided if he so wished. Matthew is perhaps trying to deal here with the tension we discovered in Mark between the conviction that suffering was inevitable and the agony of Jesus in Gethsemane when faced with death: the temptation to avoid suffering is a real one, but is resisted because scripture *must* be fulfilled.

The next significant difference from Mark occurs in Matt. 26.63f. The high priest puts Jesus under oath, and many commentators suggest that this is why Jesus refuses to give a direct reply to his challenge (see 5.33–7). But the response he makes here – 'You have said it' (*su eipas*), instead of Mark's clear 'I am' – reminds us that the high priest himself has unwittingly spoken the truth, and his attempt to impose an oath merely underlines the significance of what he has said. In the parallel scene before Pilate in 27.11, a similar dramatic device is used (as it is in Mark) when Jesus responds to Pilate's question with the words 'You say so' (*su legeis*): Jesus thus confirms the truth of what both his 'judges' say about him.

Matthew is alone among the evangelists in describing the repentance of Judas, the outcome of which is, as we have seen, the fulfilment of scripture in the purchase of the potter's field (27.3–10). In returning the thirty pieces of silver to the religious authorities, Judas declares 'I have sinned in betraying innocent blood', but they brush responsibility aside: 'What is that to us? It is your concern.'

These two themes of innocence and responsibility recur throughout this chapter. As in Mark, Pilate recognizes that the charges brought against Jesus are false, and he attempts to release him. A peculiarly Matthaean incident is found in 27.19, where Pilate's wife sends a message urging him to have nothing to do with 'that innocent (*dikaios*) man' because she has been troubled throughout the night by dreams on his account. And in 27.24–5 (again in Matthew alone) Pilate himself, yielding to the Jewish leaders' wish to have Jesus put to death, washes his hands in full view of the crowd, declaring that he is innocent of his blood and passing responsibility over to them with the words 'You see to it'. His words echo those used by the Jewish leaders themselves in 27.4, just as the terms 'innocent' and 'blood' (*athoios . . . haimatos*) echo those used by Judas. Unlike Judas, however, Jesus' accusers are happy to accept responsibility for what they are doing: in the terrible words of 27.25 they declare 'His blood be on us and on our children'. These words (found only in Matthew) are attributed to the whole people, and not just to their leaders: Matthew thus lays the blame for Jesus' death squarely upon the Jews. There is tremendous irony here: the high priest has pronounced Jesus guilty of blasphemy, which means that he falls under the curse of God; the Sanhedrin has engineered Jesus' death, and demanded that he be crucified, the form of death which would brand him as accursed.[6] But he is innocent, and in shouldering responsibility for his death the people bring the curse down on their own heads. It is important to see these words in the context of Matthew's story. For him, they are the climax of the rejection of Jesus by his own people – a theme which has run through his whole gospel. Unfortunately they have often been quoted out of context, where they have taken on a life of their own and have been interpreted as a curse on the Jewish people for all time, so providing scriptural warrant for anti-semitism. This verse, like many other passages in Matthew's gospel, reflects the bitter arguments that were taking place between Jews and Christians at the time that he was writing. Only a small minority of the Jewish people had accepted the gospel, and they had been expelled from the synagogues and were regarded by their fellow Jews as heretics; the small company of Jewish Christians, in turn, blamed the rest of their countrymen for their failure to respond to the gospel and for their rejection of their Messiah. In this situation, harsh words were said on both sides: a saying forged in this context cannot be used as justification for apportioning the blame for Jesus' death.

Matthew's account of the crucifixion is very close to Mark's, but there are significant minor changes. Matthew expands the taunts hurled at Jesus as he hangs on the cross, with the result that the emphasis shifts to his 'claim' to be the Son of God. Those who mock him urge him twice over to demonstrate that he is God's Son by saving himself from

6 Deut. 21.23.

death; their words echo those of Satan in the temptation story in 4.1–11. As there, so here, Jesus 'proves' himself to be the Son of God by renouncing power, not exercising it. At the moment of Jesus' death Matthew adds a second eschatological sign to the tearing of the temple curtain: there is an earthquake, causing graves to be opened and the bodies of many of God's saints to be raised (27.51f.). We are somewhat surprised at this last detail – we would naturally expect the resurrection of the saints to take place after Jesus himself is raised, not when he dies. Matthew himself appears to agree when he goes on to say that they came out of their graves 'after his resurrection', though it is possible that this phrase has been added by someone who was puzzled by the idea that these Old Testament 'saints' were raised *before* Jesus himself. Nevertheless, we grasp the theological point that Matthew is making: the death – and resurrection – of Jesus is a cosmic event which brings about the resurrection of God's holy people.

As in Mark, Jesus' death leads to the declaration that Jesus must have been the 'Son of God',[7] but these words seem to be a reaction to 'the earthquake and everything that was happening' which overwhelmed the onlookers with fear, rather than, as in Mark (15.39), to the way in which Jesus died. In Matthew, this confession is made by 'the centurion and those with him who were guarding Jesus', not by the centurion alone: perhaps Matthew felt that the reference to more than one witness would confirm the truth of what is said. Presumably these are the very men who are said to have mocked Jesus in 27.27–31 as 'king of the Jews'!

Matthew tells us that the tomb in which Joseph of Arimathaea (whom he describes as a disciple) placed Jesus' body was his own, and unused, the linen shroud was clean, and therefore pure: Jesus' resting-place is thus a fitting one. The fact that Joseph is described as rich (27.57) could be a fleeting echo of Isa. 53.9.

The story of the sealing of the tomb (27.62–6) is found only in Matthew. His purpose in including it is clear: rumours were circulating in his day that the disciples had stolen Jesus' body, and the story is an attempt to prove that this was not so. The narrative bears all the traces of a late development. Even if we accept the evangelists' belief that Jesus made clear predictions of his death and resurrection, we have to remember that they insist that these predictions

---

7 Here, too, the phrase is used without an article.

were made privately, to his disciples: there is no basis, therefore, for what the religious authorities tell Pilate in v. 63 – that Jesus had openly foretold his resurrection – any more than for their suggestion that the disciples, last seen fleeing from Gethsemane, were likely to steal Jesus' body and fabricate rumours of his resurrection. The details of the story are equally unlikely: the religious authorities would certainly not have come to Pilate on the sabbath, and it seems improbable that he would have been willing to provide a guard. We note the irony in Pilate's comment: 'Make the grave as secure as you can.' We who know the end of the story realize that it is impossible to make it secure, and Pilate apparently recognizes that fact!

The guards reappear in Matthew's resurrection story, first (28.2–4) as witnesses of the violent earthquake and the opening of the grave by an angel of the Lord (something which is neither observed by witnesses nor described in any of the other gospels), and secondly when they report – to the chief priests, not to Pilate! – what has happened, and are bribed to say that the disciples stole the body (28.11–15). Once again, the story is full of improbabilities: Roman soldiers (if they valued their own lives) would never have confessed to falling asleep on duty (even for 'a substantial bribe'), and it is difficult to understand how they could have claimed to observe the disciples stealing the body while they were asleep! The story is an attempt to explain the rumours that were circulating, and at the same time to blame the Jews for their refusal to acknowledge that Jesus has been raised: even when the chief priests and elders are told what has happened, they refuse to admit their error and are depicted as deliberately suppressing the truth. Matthew's narrative at this point is far removed from Mark's: Mark gave us the empty tomb and a statement, that Jesus had been raised and nothing more; Matthew here tries to establish the historical truth of the resurrection. In this incident he presents the resurrection, not as something to be accepted by faith, but as a 'fact' whose truth cannot be denied – except by those who deliberately refuse to acknowledge it.

It is in keeping with this different approach that Matthew changes Mark's abrupt ending in 16.8. Instead of rushing headlong from the tomb, too frightened to say anything, the women[8] in Matthew hurry away, fearful, but also with

---

8 Matthew mentions two: 'Mary of Magdala and the other Mary'. Salome, who is included in the group by Mark, is not mentioned.

tremendous joy, and run to tell the disciples the news (28.5–8). On the way, Jesus himself meets them, and these women are thus (surprisingly!) the first witnesses of the resurrection: the disciples do not see him until they obey his instruction to return to Galilee (28.9f.).[9]

Matthew reports two appearances of the risen Lord. The first, to the women, adds nothing to the story: Jesus merely repeats the message already given them by the angel (28.8–10). The second takes place on a mountain in Galilee, when he takes leave of the eleven disciples (28.16–20). He announces to them that he has been given full authority in heaven and on earth, and sends them out to teach and baptize in the name of the Father, the Son and the Holy Spirit: the language clearly reflects the beliefs of the later Christian community.

These two stories may well persuade us of Mark's wisdom in omitting any accounts of encounters between the risen Lord and his followers! This is an experience to be believed rather than recorded: Matthew, at least, seems to have found it difficult to express it in words. Nor is belief necessarily easy. Matthew tells us that on the mountain the eleven disciples worshipped him, but that 'some doubted' (28.17): does he mean 'some of the eleven'? A few commentators take 'some' here to refer to disciples other than the eleven, but it seems strange if another group of disciples is suddenly introduced here. Whichever way we take the passage it is significant that Matthew is not afraid, even at this point in his narrative, to say that some of the disciples had doubts – presumably about the reality of the resurrection. In spite of his attempt in 28.1–4 and 11–15 to 'prove' the resurrection as an objective 'fact' open to historical scrutiny, he acknowledges here that it is a matter of faith which can be 'tested' only by those who experience the Risen Lord. His comment here is in accord with other stories in his gospel where the disciples have been presented as men whose faith is inadequate.[10]

The changes made by Matthew to Mark's story are often minor, yet they add up to a significant shift in emphasis. We have seen how he stresses both the fulfilment of scripture and the innocence of Jesus, and how he depicts Jesus as in

---

9 Paul makes no reference to women in 1 Corinthians: either he did not know this tradition, or he did not consider women to be reliable witnesses!
10 8.26; 14.31; 16.8.

control of events. The story of Jesus' death has begun to be a story of power rather than weakness: Jesus could call on twelve legions of angels to save him if he wished (26.53); twice on the cross he is mocked as Son of God and tempted to exercise his power and save himself from death (27.40, 42); his death is accompanied by powerful signs – an earthquake, and the resurrection of the saints (27.51–3). The scandal of the cross is beginning to disappear, as Christians struggle to explain how God's power was working through it. Nevertheless, the paradox remains: the power is still exercised through weakness, since Jesus resists the temptation to save himself from death, and proves himself, by his obedient suffering, to be the Son of God.

CHAPTER FIVE

Luke-Acts

It has frequently been said, echoing the words of an influential English commentary, that Luke has 'no theology of the cross'. If we were to accept that judgement, there would be no justification for this chapter! But can it be right?

If we look more closely at the original comment, we find that it contains an important qualification: 'There is indeed no *theologia crucis* beyond the affirmation that the Christ must suffer, since so the prophetic scriptures had foretold.'[1] We have seen already that the narratives of both Mark and Matthew are dominated by the belief that Jesus had to suffer because the scriptures decreed it, so that it is hardly surprising if this same theme plays an important role in Luke also. It is important, moreover, to recognize that this affirmation is in itself an interpretation – in other words, a 'theology' – of the cross. But Professor Creed's comment was intended to point to what he felt to be a lack in Luke's gospel – to the absence of what he terms 'Pauline interpretation of the Cross', and to the fact that Luke omits crucial words from the sayings in Mark 10.45 and 14.24. How significant are these omissions?

We will return to this question in a moment, but first let us consider what Luke *does* say about Jesus' death – both in references to the fulfilment of scripture and in other ways.

We find the first hint of the passion already in 2.34f., where Simeon tells Mary that Jesus is destined to be a sign that will be rejected, and warns her that a sword will pierce her soul. This prophecy is one of a number made by Spirit-filled persons in Luke 1–2 (Mary, Zechariah, Simeon and Anna) whose words, like those of the angels and the Spirit-filled Jesus, are authoritative announcements of what will take place, and thus the equivalent of scripture. Like many

---

1 J. M. Creed, *The Gospel according to St Luke*, London 1930, p. lxxii.

of the references to scripture, this passage gives no hint as to *why* Jesus must be rejected.

A second premonition of the passion occurs in Luke 4.28–30, at the conclusion of Jesus' sermon in Nazareth. In that sermon Jesus claims that scripture has been fulfilled – the Spirit of the Lord rests upon him, and he has been anointed to carry out the tasks described in Isaiah 61. He goes on to suggest that his message will be rejected by his own people, since 'no prophet is recognized in his own country', and that, like Elijah and Elisha in times past, his mission will be to Gentiles. This idea is remarkable in itself, since Luke depicts Jesus as confining his ministry to Jews, and it is only in his second volume, Acts, that Gentiles receive the gospel. Jesus' words therefore point forward to what will happen after his death and resurrection. His words infuriate the congregation in the synagogue, who drive him out of town and attempt to lynch him, but he mysteriously escapes. The story is thus a mini-presentation of the passion narrative, with one interesting reversal: instead of Jesus' death and resurrection leading to the mission to the Gentiles, it is the suggestion that Jesus is bringing salvation to the Gentiles that rouses his countrymen's fury and leads them to attempt to kill him.

The first clear prediction of the passion occurs in Luke 9.22, the equivalent of Mark 8.31. But Luke omits Mark's comment that Jesus spoke plainly, as well as Peter's protest and Jesus' rebuke. He gives no indication here as to the disciples' reaction, but after the second and third predictions (9.44; 18.34) he emphasizes that they did not understand what Jesus was saying and that they could not grasp it because its meaning was concealed from them. Luke also omits the conversation between Jesus and his disciples which follows the transfiguration in Mark, in which Jesus points forward to the resurrection and links the sufferings of Elijah with those of the Son of man. Instead, he tells us the subject of conversation between Jesus, Moses and Elijah on the mountain: they spoke, he says, of his departure, which he was about to accomplish in Jerusalem (9.31). The term translated 'departure' is in Greek *exodus*, and though it is occasionally used elsewhere of someone's death it is not the normal term: it has clearly been used here in order to link Jesus' death with the Exodus, the great redemptive action of God which rescued his people from slavery in Egypt. This is confirmed by the fact that Jesus is said to be about to 'accomplish' or 'fulfil' it: the verb *plēroō* used here is the word used frequently in the New Testament of 'fulfilling the scriptures'. Jesus' death, then, is seen by Luke as a new Exodus, a great redemptive act whose results will presumably be parallel to those achieved by the Exodus from Egypt.

A significant turning-point takes place in Luke's narrative at 9.51, at the beginning of a long section which is usually termed the 'travel narrative'. It begins in solemn style: 'When the time approached for him to be taken up . . . .' The introductory phrase is literally 'It came to pass in the completion of the days', suggesting once again the idea of fulfilment: the time appointed had arrived. It is the time appointed for Jesus' 'assumption': the word *analēmpsis*, lit. a 'taking-up', is a rare one, but is apparently used here of Jesus being taken up to heaven. In setting out to Jerusalem, therefore, Jesus has his eyes set on the ultimate goal – not just the cross but on the vindication which lies beyond.

Luke 9.18–51 thus occupies a pivotal position in Luke's story. Within the space of a few verses, Jesus has been recognized as Messiah by Peter and declared to be Son of God by a voice from heaven; he has spoken to his disciples twice about the future sufferings of the Son of man, and has discussed his 'exodus' with Moses and Elijah on the mountain. Throughout this section the themes of glory and suffering are intertwined even more clearly than in the Markan and Matthaean parallels. Jesus is Messiah – but as the Son of man he must suffer; the Son of man will come in glory – but he will be ashamed of those who were not prepared to suffer for Jesus' sake; Jesus is revealed as God's Son in glory – while discussing the necessity for his own death; he sets out to Jerusalem – and his goal is the 'taking-up' which lies beyond the cross. Woven into this is the theme of discipleship: the disciples, like Jesus himself, must be prepared to lose their lives if they want to save them (9.23–27). This passage is almost identical with Mark 8.34ff., but Luke makes one significant addition in 9.23, where Jesus' followers are challenged to take up the cross 'daily'. The addition blunts the metaphor, since one can be crucified only once – though Paul is led to make similar exaggerated statements (Rom. 8.36; 1 Cor. 15.30f.; 2 Cor. 4.10–12). But Luke is not watering down the saying – rather he is spelling out just what renouncing self may entail: those who wish to be Jesus' followers must be prepared to accept his way of self-sacrifice as their calling.[2] They must learn, too, that

---

2 A similar emphasis is found in the saying in Luke 14.26f.

greatness belongs to those who are content to be least (9.46–48). The disciples are slow learners, however; they cannot understand Jesus' words about his own suffering (9.45), and neither do they understand their own calling, for they start arguing about which of them is the greatest (9.46). The disciples fail in another way in this section also, first in that they are unable to exorcise a demon (9.37–43), even though Jesus gave them the authority to do so in 9.1, and then because, having failed themselves, they try to prevent someone else casting out demons (9.49–50).

The juxtaposition of the first of these two stories – the healing of the epileptic child – with those of Peter's confession and the transfiguration, makes us aware that the authority over demons which Jesus possesses is of a piece with his Messiahship-through-suffering: Jesus has authority over the demons because he is the obedient Son of God who accepts God's way for him. In Luke 4, Satan tempted Jesus to prove his authority 'as Son of God' by exercising power and accepting human glory. In 9.35, Luke reminds us again that Jesus is God's Son – and immediately afterwards we are told how he defeated a minion of Satan and healed his victim (9.37–43). If the disciples fail to drive out the demon, is this because they cannot comprehend Jesus' teaching about suffering (9.43b–45) and are still hankering for human glory (9.46–48), and so are unable to exercise his authority? Luke has followed Mark's order throughout this section, but by cutting out Mark 9.9–13, 21–24, 26–29, and by adding the references to the Exodus and the taking-up, he has made the links between glory and suffering even more stark, and reminded us that what is taking place in Jesus' ministry, death and resurrection is also a defeat of Satan.[3]

We are not surprised, therefore, when we come to Luke's passion narrative, to find that Judas is in the power of Satan (22.3). Luke thus offers an explanation for Judas' behaviour – but far more important, he reminds us that through Jesus' death, Satan is being defeated. To be sure, Satan is seen here as the agent of Jesus' death, but in attempting to destroy Jesus he is in fact bringing about his own destruction.[4]

---

3 In a famous study, *The Theology of Saint Luke*, E. Tr. 1960, Hans Conzelmann argued that Satan was 'absent' from Luke's gospel between 4.13 and 22.3. It seems more accurate to say that during the ministry of Jesus he is in retreat. See 10.17f. and 11.14–20.
4 Cf. 1 Cor. 2.8.

Before that happens, however, he is at work, not simply through Judas, but also through the machinations of the Jewish leaders, for this is their hour, and 'the hour of the power of darkness' (22.53). Even the disciples are subject to Satan's attacks and will succumb to his temptations, though they will later be restored (22.31f.).

Before we come to the passion narrative itself, however, we find more ominous hints of what lies ahead in Jerusalem. 13.22 marks a half-way stage on the journey, as Luke reminds us that Jesus is travelling towards Jerusalem, and in 13.31–35 we are reminded of what will happen when he arrives. A group of Pharisees warn Jesus that Herod wants to kill him and urge him to leave his territory,[5] though their motives are not clear and Luke does not explain whether they are genuinely concerned for Jesus' safety or simply want to get rid of him. Jesus' response, enigmatic though it is, nevertheless indicates that he will not be deterred from his chosen course by Herod's wiles, which cannot in any case succeed, since 'it cannot be that a prophet should perish outside Jerusalem'. He will leave Galilee at the appointed time, and not when Herod or the Pharisees want him to. 'Today and tomorrow' – the phrase indicates that the time is limited, though imprecise – Jesus will continue his work of exorcism and healing, and on the third day he will reach his goal (*teleioumai*); this verb may perhaps mean simply 'I am completed/perfected' – in other words, 'my ministry is done'. We note once again the close link between Jesus' healings and exorcisms and his death.

This prophecy of what awaits him in Jerusalem is followed by a lament over Jerusalem – the city that 'murders the prophets and stones those who are sent to her'. Because Jerusalem has failed to respond, her temple is forsaken by God. Once again, the saying is enigmatic, but one thing is clear to us: Jerusalem has rejected God's messengers in the past, and is about to reject Jesus also.

In 18.31 we have the parallel to Mark's third prediction of the passion and resurrection, and the end of the journey is almost in sight. In 19.28–40 Jesus enters Jerusalem, hailed as king by his disciples. The Pharisees in the crowd protest, but Jesus refuses to silence his followers, and utters another

---

5 According to Luke's narrative Jesus is no longer in Galilee. Either Luke, in placing the incident here, is thinking of Jesus as in Peraea, which was also under Herod Antipas' jurisdiction, or – more likely – this is an example of his scanty geographical knowledge.

lament over the city which has failed to recognize the time of God's visitation and as a result will be razed to the ground.

After these two hints that Jesus' fate is closely linked with that of Jerusalem, we are not surprised to find that Luke spells this out very clearly in 21.20ff. Perhaps it is because he has made the link clear in other ways that he omits Mark's story of the withered fig tree – though he records a parable of a fruitless fig tree, a less dramatic story with a similar moral, in 13.6–9.

Luke also omits the story of Jesus' anointing by a woman, having already used a similar story (about a woman who anoints Jesus' *feet*) in 7.36–39. We move straight from the introductory statement that Passover was approaching (22.1f.) and the account of Judas' treachery (22.3–6) to the preparations for the meal (22.7–13) and the account of the meal itself (22.14–38). There are several remarkable things about Luke's version of the Last Supper. Jesus begins by telling the disciples how he has longed to eat this Passover before he suffers, and though the form of the saying suggests that his wish remains unfulfilled, in the context Luke has given it he presumably thinks that the meal in the upper room is a Passover. But the emphasis lies on future expectation: Jesus will not eat the Passover again until the meal finds its fulfilment in the Kingdom of God (v. 16). In a parallel saying in 22.17f. he says that he will not drink wine again until the Kingdom of God comes. Jesus tells the disciples to take the cup he offers them and divide it among themselves, and we are left wondering whether Luke means that Jesus himself abstained. Did he think of Jesus as sharing in the meal or merely presiding? Perhaps the hints that he did not himself eat and drink reflect the beliefs of the Christian community that the meal is now symbolic of his death. It is at any rate clear that when Jesus declares that he will not share in the Passover or drink wine until the Kingdom of God is here, he expresses his confidence in God's final vindication; moreover, in stressing that he will not eat or drink again, while telling the disciples to share the cup, there is a hint that responsibility has now passed to them.

One of the strange features of Luke's account of the Last Supper is that the cup is passed round before the bread. In many mss, however, this is then followed by a *second* cup, while others break off after the words 'This is my body'. There is much debate about whether the shorter or the longer text is the original. The disputed passage, 22.19b–20, is close to what we find in Mark and Matthew, though it adds the idea (found also in Paul) that the bread is shared as a 'memorial' of Jesus.

Another remarkable feature of Luke's narrative is the dispute between the disciples that takes place in 22.24–30, immediately after Jesus has spoken about his betrayer (vv. 21–23). At this solemn moment, when Jesus has been talking to his disciples about his death, they start arguing about which of them is the greatest! Nevertheless, Jesus' response is entirely appropriate to the context: 'Who is greater?' he asks, 'The one who sits at table, or the one who serves? Surely it is the one who sits at table. But I am among you as one who serves.' The passage is parallel to the one we find in Mark 10.42–45, but the bare reference to Jesus serving others replaces the famous saying in Mark 10.45: 'For even the Son of man came not to be served but to serve and to give his life a ransom for many.'

As we saw at the beginning of this chapter, some commentators have considered Luke's omission of the Markan saying at this point to be extremely significant. Certainly it seems strange that he did not use it, for the reference to Jesus' death would be highly relevant at this point. But did he *deliberately* reject it? It is important to recognize that in much of the passion narrative Luke seems to be following a tradition other than Mark's, and in this section (22.24–30) he is certainly not using Mark, since both the setting and the wording are very different from Mark's. But if Luke is here following a non-Markan tradition, why should we expect him to remember that Mark has used a similar story in another context or consider it necessary to add bits of the Markan version to his account? Would Luke not have been astonished to be told that he had deliberately cut out the saying about Jesus' death being a ransom for others? Moreover, if we read on in Luke's story, we find that the suggestion that Luke might have 'objected' to Mark's saying is contradicted by Jesus' next words. Jesus has already told the disciples that they must not take Gentile kings as their model (v. 25); the example he offers them is his own (v. 27). Now he goes on to describe the community in which they seek to be great as *his* kingdom, and says that he is entrusting to them the kingdom which his Father had entrusted to him. So by his death Jesus makes his disciples sharers in his kingdom: they will eat and drink at his table, and rule over the twelve tribes of Israel. The language may be different from the famous saying in Mark 10.45 about the Son of man giving his life as a ransom for many, but the *meaning* is very close indeed.

One remarkable feature of Jesus' promise here is that it is made to the disciples on the basis of the fact that they have stood firmly by him in his times of trial. The irony of the words at this point in the story is striking, for they are addressed to men who are about to desert Jesus – as the very next saying, in 22.31–4, points out! The promise accords with Jesus' earlier challenges to his disciples to renounce themselves, shoulder the cross and follow him, and with the assurances that those who do so will be recognized by the Son of man.[6] Up to this point in the narrative, of course, the disciples *have* (with the exception of Judas, whose betrayal is predicted immediately before this) remained loyal to Jesus. In Matthew, the promise that the disciples will rule the tribes of Israel forms part of Jesus' response to Peter when he reminds Jesus that the disciples have left everything to follow him.[7] In using the saying here, Luke had to solve a problem: how could the promise be addressed to the disciples, *excluding Judas*? His solution was to omit the word 'twelve' before 'thrones', but the 'twelve' before 'tribes' remains. In its Lukan context, the saying does three things: first, it underlines the failure of the disciples, who in the event fail to stand firm; second, it is a challenge to would-be disciples to remain loyal to Jesus throughout the times of trial, and not to succumb to Satan's temptations, as did the twelve; third, knowing the rest of the story as we do, it is a hint that there is forgiveness and renewal, even for those who deny Jesus and run away: his promise stands, in spite of human weakness and failure.

The scene in the upper room ends with a conversation which contrasts the welcome given to Jesus' disciples during his ministry with the enmity that confronts them now. Conditions have changed – now they need not only money to support themselves, but swords to defend themselves. These words presumably reflect the realities of discipleship in the post-resurrection period. The experience of the disciples is linked here to that of their Lord: they will be treated as evil-doers because that is how he is treated, and this is because the words of scripture have to be fulfilled, namely that 'he was reckoned among transgressors' – treated, that is, as a common criminal. The response of the

---

6 Luke 9.23–6; 12.8f. 14.27; 18.28–30.
7 Matt. 19.27–30; cf. Luke 18.28–30.

disciples, who (somewhat surprisingly!) produce two swords, together with Jesus' enigmatic reply – 'Enough!' – indicate their total incomprehension.

This is the only occasion in the synoptic gospels on which an explicit quotation from Isaiah 53 is applied to the death of Jesus – a remarkable fact, since to us this is the passage of scripture which above any other appears to be an appropriate description of the meaning of Jesus' sufferings. Even more remarkable is the fact that the quotation here is in no way applied to the *significance* of his death, but simply to the fact that he was put to death in the company of malefactors. When we remember that on the only other occasion in the gospels on which an explicit quotation from Isaiah 53 is used – in Matt. 8.17 – it refers to Jesus' acts of healing, we begin to realize that the early Christian communities did not always use scripture in the ways that seem to us to be obvious and appropriate! Luke's use of Isaiah 53 at this point, without drawing out the passage's deeper theological significance, is another reason why some commentators have regarded Luke as lacking a 'theology of the cross'. But since the other evangelists do not quote the passage at all, he cannot be understood as rejecting anything. It is better to recognize what Luke *has* done, rather than criticizing him for not interpreting the passage in the way we expect. What we have here is an example of the way in which the early Christian community searched the scriptures and interpreted them as having been fulfilled in the life, death and resurrection of Jesus.

The story of Jesus' prayer in the Garden of Gethsemane (22.39–46) is similar to what we read in Mark and Matthew, but it is much shorter, since in Luke's account Jesus retreats to pray only once. The description of Jesus' agony in 22.43f. is unique to Luke: an angel appears from heaven in order to support Jesus, and sweat falls from him like drops of blood. But these two verses are missing from many early mss, and are almost certainly a late addition to the text. They remind us of the reality of the struggle: in spite of the evangelists' insistence that Jesus 'had' to die, the possibility of avoiding the cup of suffering was a real option at the time.

Luke's account of Judas' betrayal (22.47f.) is also much briefer than those in Matthew and Mark, since he omits the arrangement between Judas and the authorities, and it is by no means clear whether Judas actually kisses Jesus, or whether Jesus prevents him. But Luke *has* told us that the disciples possess two swords, so that we are not unduly surprised when they produce one. Only Luke tells us that Jesus healed the man's ear: since this had been cut off, the detail appears to be a naive legendary addition, but perhaps Luke means no more than that Jesus staunched the flow of blood. In either case, the incident demonstrates the salvific power of Jesus, even toward those who are determined to destroy him.

Much of the material that follows is similar to that found in Mark and Matthew, though events are recounted in a different order. First Luke deals with Peter (22.54–62), which means that the stories of Judas' betrayal and Peter's denial are told in close proximity; nothing is said about the desertion of the other disciples. Then we are told about the mockery by Jesus' guards (22.63–5); this occupies the rest of the night. Luke is perhaps aware of the historical problems in Mark's reference to a night session of the Sanhedrin: at any rate, Luke tells us that the meeting took place at first light. He says nothing about the charges and witnesses mentioned in Mark and Matthew, and goes straight to the question posed by the high priest as to whether Jesus was the Messiah. Jesus' response is indirect: 'If I tell you.' he says, 'You will not believe me; and if I question you, you will not reply. But from now on the Son of man will be seated at the right hand of the power of God.' When the members of the Sanhedrin ask him 'Are you the Son of God then?' he replies 'You have said that I am'. What does Luke intend us to understand by these enigmatic words? They are hardly a clear affirmative reply. Yet Jesus' questioners certainly treat them as affirmative. The form of wording throws the responsibility back onto his interrogators – 'It is you yourselves who have said what I am'. As in Mark and Matthew, the truth about Jesus is found in the mouth of Jesus' accusers, who refuse to accept that it is the truth.

In the very next scene (23.1–5), Jesus makes a very similar response to Pilate when the latter asks him whether he is king of the Jews, but this time his reply is not taken seriously, and Pilate decides to dismiss the case. Luke now adds a story that is not found in the other gospels (23.6–12): Pilate tries to get rid of the problem by sending Jesus to Herod, on the pretext that, as a Galilean, Jesus fell under his jurisdiction, but Herod, after attempting to interrogate Jesus and mocking him as an imposter, sends him back to Pilate. The story serves to confirm the innocence of Jesus: neither Pilate nor Herod considers the charges brought against Jesus by the Jewish leaders to have any foundation (23.13–16) but, as in the other gospels, the leaders force Pilate's arm and get their way. At this point in the story Luke suggests, even more clearly than do Mark and Matthew, that Barabbas is released *instead of* Jesus. He makes no attempt, as they do, to explain why the Jewish people might expect the Roman prefect to release any of his prisoners, so that the demand in v. 18 comes out of the blue: 'Away with this man! Release to us Barabbas!' Though Barabbas is irrelevant to the accusations made against Jesus, and though Pilate protests that Jesus himself is innocent, he nevertheless releases Barabbas and 'hands over Jesus (the verb is once again *paradidōmi*) to their will. Thus the way in which Luke tells the story points us to its theological significance: the one who has done no wrong dies in place of the man who has been justly convicted as worthy of death.

Luke's account of the crucifixion is punctuated by passages which have no parallel in the other gospels. The first comes in 23.27–31: as Jesus leaves the city, he is accompanied by a large crowd, and by women lamenting his fate, whom Jesus warns of the still worse fate that is to come on them and on their children. We are reminded of the occasion when Jesus rode into the city, accompanied by another crowd, and wept over Jerusalem, predicting its coming destruction. Once again we see the link in the evangelist's mind between the rejection of Jesus by the Jerusalem hierarchy and the city's destruction, which is interpreted as her punishment.

The second addition is found at 23.34, where Jesus prays for his executioners: 'Father, forgive them, for they do not know what they are doing'. The words are missing from many mss and may well be an early addition to the text, but if so they accord well with Luke's approach. The notion that those who put Jesus to death were unaware of what they were doing is found again in Acts 3.17; 13.27, and throughout both Luke and Acts there is constant emphasis on the theme of forgiveness.

The third addition is found in 23.39–43. In Mark and Matthew, both the criminals executed with Jesus taunt him, but in Luke only one of them does so, while the other acknowledges his own guilt and points out that Jesus has done nothing wrong: once again we are reminded of Jesus' innocence. The man asks Jesus to remember him when he enters his kingdom. Whether Luke thinks of the words as spoken wistfully or seriously is not clear and in any case unimportant, since in this context they are an implicit christological confession, similar to that uttered by the centurion in Mark: Jesus is now at the point of death – yet this man speaks of him entering into his kingdom! Here is faith indeed, and his faith is instantly rewarded by Jesus' promise: 'Today you will be with me in Paradise'. There is no need to wait for some future 'coming' of the Son of man to earth, since 'from now on the Son of man will be seated at the right hand of the power of God' (22.69). If the criminal's words are an implicit recognition of who Jesus is, Jesus' response is an indication of the salvation and forgiveness which he offers to those who repent.

In Mark and Matthew, Jesus' last words are taken from the opening verses of Psalm 22 (Mark 15.34; Matt. 27.46). Luke tells us that his final words echoed a verse from Psalm 31 expressing confidence in God, and so avoids the suggestion that he died in despair. The centurion, 'seeing what happened', responded, not (as in Mark and Matthew) with a confession that Jesus is Son of God, but with the declaration that he must have been innocent. So now Pilate, Herod, one of the men who shared Jesus' death and his executioner have all declared him to be innocent. What was it that the centurion saw? Presumably Luke is thinking of the eclipse (vv. 44f.) and the manner of Jesus' death. The statement in v. 47 that he glorified God strikes one as absurd: why should he praise God that an innocent man has been put to death in this barbaric way? The words point to the hidden irony in the story: to human eyes, what has happened looks like utter disaster, but to the eyes of faith it is a cause for praising God. In contrast to the centurion, the crowd which had gathered for the spectacle, presumably expecting to enjoy it, went home beating their breasts, though whether this was because they recognized that an innocent man had been put to death or because, having witnessed the eclipse, they now expected retribution, is not clear.

Like the other evangelists, Luke tells of the visit of the women to the tomb on Easter Sunday morning, but the two angels who meet them there do not tell them to send the disciples to Galilee, and the appearances of the Risen Lord take place in or near Jerusalem. The heavenly messengers remind the women that Jesus himself had spoken of his betrayal, death and resurrection. This scene at the empty tomb is the first of three in which Luke is able to remind his readers that the death and resurrection of Jesus were foretold, not simply by scripture, but by Jesus himself. This is the substance of the angels' words to the women, who report them to the disciples – but the men refuse to believe them.

The slowness of Jesus' followers to believe that he has been raised is a constant theme in this final chapter in Luke. In the second scene (24.13–32), Jesus meets two of them as they travel to Emmaus. 'How dull you are!' he exclaims. 'How slow to believe all that the prophets said! Was not the Messiah bound to suffer in this way before entering into his glory?' He then, says Luke, spelt out this theme to them 'from the whole of scripture'.

In the final scene, the two travellers rush back to Jerusalem, and are greeted by the news that the Lord has appeared to Simon. But when Jesus himself appears among them the disciples think that he is a ghost, whereupon he upbraids them for their lack of faith (24.36–43). This time he reminds them of his own teaching as well as that of scripture, since he had explained to them, he says, how everything written about him in the law and the prophets and psalms had to be fulfilled (24.44–6).

By including conversations between the Risen Lord and the disciples, Luke is able to spell out the significance of what had taken place in a way that Matthew and Mark were unable to do. His narrative thus helps us to understand the way in which the Christian community thought out the implications of its faith during the earliest period. The emphasis given to the theme of fulfilment throughout these resurrection scenes reflects the experience of the earliest believers. As they pored over their scriptures and recalled the words of Jesus they understood them in a new way: 'so that's what it means (*or* what he meant)!' they must have exclaimed, again and again. The doubts and fears of the disciples, too, would often be shared by Christians who had not seen the Risen Lord. In Luke's narrative, it is only the women who apparently have no doubts, and who accept the angels' message without even meeting Jesus (vv. 6–10)! The disciples refuse to believe their story (24.11), the two travellers fail to recognize Jesus throughout their journey (24.16), and the company in Jerusalem have doubts and are incredulous (24.38, 41). Like the other evangelists, Luke freely acknowledges the difficulty of believing in the truth of the resurrection.

The fact that the eyes of Cleopas and his companion were opened when Jesus broke bread and offered it to them would also correspond with the experience of the early communities. For them, fellowship meals were certainly of great importance[8] and were occasions, not simply to meet with fellow-Christians, but to celebrate the presence of the Risen Lord.

Finally, we find indications in this chapter of the ways in which Luke's community interpreted and understood the death and resurrection of Jesus. 'Was it not necessary,' asks Jesus of Cleopas and his companion, 'that the Messiah should suffer these things and so enter into his glory?' We have already met this idea that Jesus' death is a path to glory in 9.51. But what, we want to know, did his death and resurrection *achieve*? Perhaps the answer is given us in 24.47, where the Risen Lord tells the disciples that in his name they are to preach repentance and the forgiveness of sins to all the nations: what Jesus himself proclaimed during his ministry[9] is now available for all – through his death *and resurrection*.

* * *

In this final chapter of his gospel, Luke helps his readers to look back on the death of Jesus and to see its true meaning with the eyes of faith. But Luke, alone among the evangelists, has a second opportunity – in the Acts of the Apostles – of spelling out how the death and resurrection of Jesus were now understood. In the early chapters of Acts we find a series of speeches, attributed to Peter, which summarize the Christian gospel, and central to them all is the theme of Jesus' death and resurrection. Three points are made: first, 'you' (the audience, i.e. the Jews) are responsible for his death, having handed him over to Pilate with the demand that he crucify him;[10] second, God raised him from the dead – in confirmation of which, appeal is made, either to scripture or to the apostles as witnesses;[11] third, in his name, forgiveness and salvation are now offered to those who repent.[12] In chapter 13, Paul is said to have made the same points in a sermon in the synagogue at Pisidian Antioch.[13]

It is noticeable that in all these passages, the emphasis is on the resurrection, for while Jesus' death is said to be in

---

8 Acts 2.42, 46; 20.7.
9 Luke 4.18; 5.20; 7.47–50; 15; 19.1–10.
10 Acts 2.23; 3.13f.; 4.10f.; 5.30; 10.39.
11 2.24–32; 3.15; 4.10f.; 5.30; 10.40f.
12 2.38f.; 3.19–21; 4.12; 5.31; 10.43.
13 13.28f., 30–7, 38f.

accordance with God's plan or with what the prophets foretold[14] – though where is not specified – the resurrection is described as the direct action of God himself, reversing what men have done: Jesus is now enthroned as Christ and Lord, leader and saviour.[15] The forgiveness and salvation offered in Jesus' name seem to stem from this, rather than from his death.[16] These passages correspond with the pattern set out in Luke 24.26: it was necessary for the Christ to suffer before he could enter into his glory.

There are two passages in Acts, however, which refer to the death of Jesus without specifically mentioning the resurrection. The first is found in 8.26–40, where the Ethiopian eunuch is said to have been reading from Isaiah 53. Remarkably, the section of that chapter that is quoted – part of vv. 7–8 – breaks off just before the statement that the righteous one who suffers unjustly is put to death for the transgressions of others. The passage is used as a simple proof-text, showing that the prophets spoke beforehand of the sufferings of the Messiah, but there is no hint of the rich theological meaning to be found in that passage. Knowing as we do the centuries-long tradition which has taken the description of *vicarious* suffering in Isaiah 53 as a prophecy of the atoning death of Christ, we are surprised that Luke apparently ignores this theme. We have to remember, however, that he associates salvation with the whole ministry of Jesus, and that the message of repentance and forgiveness proclaimed by the apostles arises from the fact that Jesus has been *raised* from the dead.

The second reference to Christ's death occurs in Acts 20.28, where Paul is said to have urged the elders at Miletus to 'care for the church of God, which he obtained for himself through the blood of his Own'.[17] The word 'blood' is used here as a synonym for 'death': it is to the death of

---

14 2.23; 3.18; 13.27, 29.

15 2.36; 5.31.

16 The theme of the resurrection is also central in Paul's speech at Athens in 17.18, 22–34. So, too, 26.23. Cf. also 23.6–10 and 24.10–21, though here the issue is the general resurrection, rather than the resurrection of Christ himself.

17 There is a difficult textual problem here. Some mss read 'the church of the Lord', in which case the final phrase is understood in its more natural sense as meaning 'his own blood'. The alternative reading, 'the church of God', is the more difficult (and therefore perhaps more likely to be the original) because it involves understanding the Greek word *idios* as meaning 'his Own [Son]'. It has to be added that though Paul himself uses

Christ that the Church owes its existence. We have met the idea that a new community is established through Jesus' death already, in Luke 22.28–30 and 23.42f. If it is unusual to find a reference to his death without any mention of the resurrection, this is perhaps partly explained by the fact that in this passage Paul is contemplating his own future sufferings and death, and also the trials which are going to come on the Christian community he is leaving behind.

Reference to Paul's own sufferings reminds us, finally, of another way in which Luke, alone among the evangelists, is able to draw out the implications of Jesus' teaching about his sufferings and death. All the evangelists tell us that Jesus warned his disciples that if they were to follow him they must be prepared to share his fate: Luke alone is able to show how they did in fact do so. Thus we read how Peter and John, Paul and Silas are thrown into prison;[18] how Paul and Silas are flogged;[19] how Stephen is stoned to death and how James, brother of John, is beheaded.[20] At other times, the apostles have to flee for their lives.[21] Nor are 'ordinary' Christians immune from attack.[22] Luke and his readers are in no danger of falling into the heresy that supposes that the sufferings and death of Christ secure his followers from danger and pain, suffering and disaster. The joy that they experience comes to them only because they are prepared to take up the cross and follow their master on the road to Calvary.

---

the expression 'the church of God' in his epistles, the alternative phrase, 'the church of the Lord', is not found elsewhere in the New Testament, though it does occur in the LXX.

18 Acts 5.17f.; 12.3–5; 16.23.
19 16.22f.
20 7.57–60; 12.2.
21 9.23–25; 14.5f.; 17.5–10. Cf. 21.30–36; 23.12–30.
22 8.1; 9.1–2; 22.19; 18.17.

CHAPTER SIX

John

Each of our evangelists had a different story to tell. Each of them had his own understanding of the significance of the events, and each had different problems to face. Each selected the material and arranged it in a way that would help his community see what the gospel meant for them. We have looked at the way in which Matthew and Luke handle the story, and noticed how each of them, while making use of the same material as Mark, underlines different aspects of what Christ's death means for Christian believers. When we turn to the Fourth Gospel we find a very different account, based on an independent tradition. It will be helpful to examine the way in which this author tells the story.

John's narrative, like that in the other gospels, finds its climax on Golgotha, but the story he tells before we reach the cross is very different. John has selected different material, and presents it in a different way, which means that though we meet familiar themes, they are expressed in different modes. Where, for example, are the passion predictions which played such an important part in the lead-up to Mark's passion narrative? John does not include them. Instead, we find Jesus announcing that the Son of man must be lifted up.[1] But surely these sayings *are* the passion predictions in a different form! Like them, they refer to what will happen to the Son of man, but instead of referring to his death and resurrection, they say that he will be lifted up. Now the verb *hupsoō* which is used here is as ambiguous in Greek as it is in English, for it is easy to see that it can refer both to Jesus being lifted up on the cross and to his exaltation in glory. In looking at Mark, I suggested that perhaps we should not speak about passion predictions, because these sayings refer to Jesus' resurrection as well as to his death. Almost invariably, Mark follows every reference

1 3.14; 8.28; 12.32 and 34.

to the Son of man's suffering with an affirmation of his future vindication; conversely, references to the Son of man's future glory acknowledge the necessity for the suffering which comes first. The two ideas of suffering and glory are held together in the synoptic tradition: as the Risen Jesus expresses it in Luke's gospel, 'the Messiah had to suffer and so enter glory.' But what has happened in John is that the two ideas have coalesced, so that one verb now sums up the ideas which in Mark were spelt out in two. The Son of man will be lifted up – first in death and then in glory. The result of this is that the death of Jesus is being presented to us in a very positive light: Jesus' death is seen as a lifting-up – an exaltation. The horror of Mark's stark references to death and to crucifixion is blunted, and we are a long way now from sharing the anguish of the disciples on the first Good Friday. John is of course recording Jesus' words with the benefit of hindsight, and instead of remembering how the despair and pain which Jesus' death caused at the time were followed by the jubilation of his resurrection, he thinks of death and resurrection together, as the saving activity of God. He interprets the lifting-up on the cross – the exposure of Jesus' naked body – in the light of the glory which was to follow. It is a bold stroke to describe this in terms of exaltation!

This is not the only way in which Jesus refers to his coming death in the Fourth Gospel. He speaks also, especially in the Farewell Discourses, of going to the Father,[2] which means that once again, his death is being seen in the light of what follows, and is simply the means by which he returns to God. Even more startling is the way in which he refers to his death as his glorification: as with the verb *hupsoō*, so with *doxazō*, to glorify,[3] we seem to have two opposites which have coalesced – the glory superimposed upon the shame, the exaltation on the death; but this time there is no question of our verb being ambiguous, for *doxazō* certainly means 'to glorify'. It is as well to remember, however, that when we speak about the glory of God we are in fact speaking about the disclosure of his nature,[4] which means that in his death, Jesus glorifies God and he himself is glorified; in other words, we see here the nature of God, and the nature of his Son. The glory of God

---

2 13.3, 33, 36; 14.4, 5, 28; 16.5, 10, 17. See also 7.33ff. and 8.21f.
3 7.39; 12.16, 23, 13.31; 17.1.
4 See 8.54; 11.4; 12.28; 13.31f.; 14.13; 15.8; 16.14; 17.1, 4f., 10.

is revealed – not, as we might suppose, in the resurrection, but in the shame of the cross.

It is hardly surprising, then, that in the Fourth Gospel Jesus speaks about his death from the very beginning. As early as 2.4, he says that his hour has not yet come – in other words, the hour of his glorification (cf. 2.11); so, too, in 7.6–8, 30; but finally, in Jerusalem, he announces that his hour has come (12.23, 27). These statements replace the appeals to the scriptures which we find in the synoptic passion predictions, but like them, they convey the idea of the divine plan, for the hour is set by God. But they also suggest that Jesus controls his own destiny, since it is *his* hour. He knows that the Jews are plotting his death (7.1, 19f.; 8.37, 40), and he knows from the beginning that Judas will betray him (6.70): but no-one can do anything until Jesus' hour arrives. The good shepherd lays down his life for his sheep (10.11, 17f.) and he does so deliberately, for no-one takes his life from him. Notice the way in which John handles the story of Judas: instead of telling us how Judas went to the authorities and offered his services; we are told that Jesus knew that Judas would betray him (13.10f., 18f.), that he singled him out and even sent him off to make arrangements for the arrest, (13.21–30): Judas may be a devil, but what he does is part of the divine plan and the fulfilment of scripture (v. 18), and since John believes Jesus to have been totally in control, even of his own death, he understands Jesus to accept and authorize, as it were, the treachery of Judas. The verb for 'betray', used again and again in the story, is the familiar *paradidōmi*.[5]

Perhaps this is why he does not include the story of Jesus in Gethsemane, for it is difficult to reconcile that tradition with the picture of Jesus in control, aware from the very beginning of his ministry that the divine plan must lead him to the cross. There is an echo of the Gethsemane story in chapter 12, however, where Jesus prays: 'Now is my soul troubled; and what shall I say? Father, save me from this hour?' Immediately he rejects the thought, however: 'No, for this purpose I have come to this hour.' This is not a struggle, as in Mark's account of Gethsemane (and even more in Luke's); rather, it is a reminder that Jesus is fully in accord with the will of God.

'For this purpose I have come to this hour': but what was the purpose of Jesus' death? This is set out in what is perhaps

---

5 6.64, 71; 12.4; 13.2, 11, 21; 18.2, 5; 21.20.

the most famous passage in the gospel, in 3.16f.: 'God so loved the world that he gave his only Son, so that whoever believes in him should not perish but have eternal life; for God sent his Son into the world, not to condemn the world, but that the world might be saved through him.' If we leave aside the contrasting negative phrases, we see that the introductory statement that God loved the world leads to two balancing clauses:

1 He gave his only Son, in order that those who believe in him might have life.
2 He sent his Son, in order that the world might be saved through him.

Now these two statements echo passages in Paul, some of which we have looked at, where he speaks either of God giving his Son or sending his Son[6] in order to restore men and women to fellowship with himself. Here John combines the two ideas of 'sending' and 'giving' – what *we* would describe, technically, as 'incarnation' and 'atonement': the coming of Jesus and the dying of Jesus belong together in God's purpose for mankind.

But how does this salvation 'work'? This is something which John never really explains, though he does provide us with a few clues, the first of which comes in the opening chapter. In the Fourth Gospel, John the Baptist recognizes Jesus from the beginning, and points him out as 'the Lamb of God who takes away the sin of the world.'[7] But what sort of lamb does the evangelist have in mind? Four suggestions have been made. The first (made by C. H. Dodd)[8] is that 'the Lamb' was a recognized messianic title; but there is little evidence to support this suggestion, and it does not explain why this lamb should take away sins. The second is that it refers to the Passover lamb; this seems much more likely, since – as we have already noted – in the Fourth Gospel Jesus dies at the very moment that the Passover lambs were slain. There is just one drawback, and that is that the Passover lamb did not remove sin either: the original Passover lambs were sacrificed in order to ward off God's

---

6 Rom. 4.25; 8.32; 8.3f.; Gal. 4.4f.
7 1.29, 36.
8 *Historical Tradition in the Fourth Gospel*, Cambridge 1963, pp. 269–71.

angel, and the annual festival is a reminder of this salvation. A third suggestion traces the lamb to Isa. 53.7, where the Servant of God is said to be like a lamb led to the slaughter; Isaiah 53 goes on to interpret these sufferings as 'for our sins'. And finally, it is possible that the evangelist was thinking of the sin-offering, for this sacrifice could be a lamb, and was certainly intended to deal with sin.

Which of these explanations is the correct one? I suspect that had we been able to ask the evangelist himself, he might have found it difficult to choose between them. For in the course of his Gospel he sets out to show how Jesus fulfils and replaces all the festivals and ceremonies of Judaism.[9] All of them point forward to him – just as the Jewish law points forward to him. If Jewish scriptures and Jewish worship point forward to Jesus and find their fulfilment in him, we can expect him to fulfil every lamb in Judaism. But to justify that statement, we need to read on through John's gospel.

In 2. 13–22 we meet a familiar story – it is the so-called 'cleansing' of the temple, which leads up to Jesus' saying about the destruction of the temple and its rebuilding. Mark places the story at the end of his gospel, immediately before the passion narrative: indeed, we have seen how it is the event which leads to Jesus' arrest and death. John places it at the very beginning of his gospel. We do not need to argue about which author has placed the story in the correct historical position. Each of them is more concerned to understand the significance of the story, and we would be wise to do the same, for each of them has important theological truth to tell us. For John, also, the story links up with the death of Jesus: challenged by the Jews to provide a sign to justify his behaviour, Jesus replies 'Destroy this temple, and in three days I will raise it up'. We may well be perplexed to understand how these words provide any kind of sign, but fortunately John explains by telling us that when Jesus was raised from the dead, the disciples remembered – and understood – the saying. In other words, the sign Jesus offers is that of his own resurrection. The saying, then, is apparently not about the temple at all, but about Jesus' own body: his enemies will destroy it, but he will rise again.

John has taken a tradition which is familiar to us from the

---

9 John's narrative is woven around the various festivals: Passover in 2.13, 6.4, 13.1; 'one of the Jewish festivals', 5.1; Tabernacles, 7.2; Dedication, 10.22. The various miracles and discourses pick up themes connected with the festivals and show how they are all fulfilled in Jesus.

Synoptics, but he has spelt out its implications in a way which the other evangelists do not do. Whereas Mark tells us that false witnesses accused Jesus of threatening to destroy the temple and rebuild it, and leaves us to work out what Jesus really did say, and what it meant, John supplies us with both the saying and the interpretation. But the saying is not simply about the death and resurrection of Jesus, for it forms the climax of Jesus' actions in the temple, and supplies the authority for those actions. Though Jesus is understood to be referring to the temple of his body, his words are nevertheless clearly relevant to what takes place in the temple at Jerusalem. Just as Mark linked the death of Jesus with the destruction of the temple, so does John – indeed, in a sense he identifies them. Why?

This story comes, as we have seen, almost at the beginning of John's gospel, immediately following the story of Jesus changing the water into wine at Cana. Both actions of Jesus are signs – signs of the new life and the new worship which Jesus brings. The water which Jesus changes into wine was intended for the Jewish rites of purification, but in his presence it is changed into the heady wine of the Gospel. The worship of Judaism is condemned by Jesus and brought to a standstill; the temple is to be destroyed and replaced by a new one – the temple of his body – so that from now on worship is to be centred on the risen Lord, not on the temple in Jerusalem. The implications of this are spelt out in the conversation between Jesus and the Samaritan woman in chapter 4: men and women will no longer worship God in Jerusalem, because they will worship him through the Spirit of truth – the Spirit who is to come when Jesus is glorified (7.39). And it is the death of Jesus which brings about this dramatic change. John tells us that Jesus hesitates to change the water into wine because his hour had not yet come – the hour, that is, of his glorification, his death. What happens in Cana, then, points forward to his death; no wonder John comments: 'this sign Jesus did at Cana in Galilee, and manifested his glory'. At Passover (the season when Jesus is later to die) he goes to Jerusalem, and his actions in the temple point forward both to his death and the temple's destruction, since one inevitably brings about the other. But beyond Jesus' death we are promised resurrection, new wine, a new community.

In placing these two stories at the beginning of his gospel, John has made it quite clear to us that Jesus is not only the fulfilment of Jewish worship, but that he inaugurates something much greater – so much greater that it can only be described as being on another plane altogether. The water-pots and the temple in Jerusalem belong to the old way of life, but to experience the new way of life which Jesus brings is like being born from above. In the story of Jesus' meeting with Nicodemus we have the account of another conversation, this time between Jesus and a respected leader of the Jewish people, but like the Samaritan woman, Nicodemus thinks in the old ways and cannot grasp what Jesus is talking about. The life which Jesus offers is available to those who believe in him – because the Son of man has been lifted up on the cross. Once again we have a reference to the death of Jesus, which is the means by which we move from old to new, but this time, his 'exaltation' on the cross is compared with the way in which the bronze serpent was lifted up by Moses, an action which saved the Israelites who had been bitten by earthly serpents,[10] another reminder that the Old Testament points forward to what happens in Christ.

In John's gospel, the event which causes the priests and Pharisees to plot together to destroy Jesus is the raising of Lazarus. There is an irony in the sequence of events which is not lost on our evangelist: Jesus raises another man from the dead, and immediately his own fate is sealed. When his enemies meet together, Caiaphas remarks: 'It is expedient that one man should die for the people, and that the whole nation should not perish' (11.50). It is clear from the context that his words are intended to apply to political expediency, for if Jesus is allowed to continue unhindered, there is a danger that the occupying Roman power will be alarmed and will send troops who will destroy both the temple and the nation: here is more irony, for that in fact is what eventually happens. But there is further irony still in Caiaphas' words, 'it is expedient that one man should die for the nation'. Here we have the familiar word *huper* – 'for': Jesus' dies for the whole nation. But what does his death achieve? He is to die 'so that the whole nation should not perish.' Compare these words with the saying in 3.16: 'God . . . gave his only Son, that whoever believes in him should not perish.' Clearly John believes that Caiaphas has spoken more truly than he knows; so significant are his words that we are reminded of them, later in the story, at 18.14. But meanwhile he adds a 'footnote', as it were to Caiaphas'

10 John 3.14; Num. 21.9.

words: Jesus died, he says, not for the nation of Israel alone, but in order to gather into one all the children of God.

This is not the only place where we find the death of Jesus linked with salvation for the Gentiles. In chapter 10, the statement that the good shepherd lays down his life for the sheep is followed by the comment: 'I have other sheep, that are not of this fold; I must bring them also.' And in 12.20ff., we have the story of the Greeks who come to Philip with the request that they should see Jesus; when Jesus is told about them, he says that the hour has come for him to be glorified, and speaks about a grain of wheat which falls into the ground and dies in order to bear fruit. Nothing more is said about the Greeks, who are apparently left standing outside! Presumably we are to understand that they can 'see' Jesus only through his death; that will be the means by which the Gentiles will be brought into the people of God.

But if Jesus' death brings salvation, it also brings judgement. The purpose of God's sending and giving of his Son, we are told in John 3.16f., is not to condemn the world but to save it. The theme is repeated in 12.44ff.: 'I did not come to judge the world but to save the world.' Nevertheless, his coming inevitably brings condemnation: 'and this is the judgement, that the light has come into the world and men loved darkness rather than light' (3.19). Their preference for darkness is seen throughout the Gospel, where Jesus and his opponents are constantly in conflict. In the Synoptics, Jesus' opponents are the scribes and Pharisees, but in John they are regularly referred to as 'the Jews'. It is an odd description, remembering that Jesus himself and the disciples were also Jews! But by the time John was writing the opposition between Jews and Christians (whether Jewish or Gentile) had become extremely bitter, and the Jewish people, by and large, had rejected the Christian message. In rejecting salvation, they inevitably fall under judgement, but it is not simply men and women who fall under judgement, for this is a conflict between good and evil, between darkness and light. The conflict comes to a head in the passion: this is the hour of judgement (12.31). This final scene in the drama is seen as a personal battle between the ruler of this world and one whose kingdom does not belong to this world. So in 12.31 we are told that the hour has come for the ruler of this world to be cast out; in 14.30, referring to his coming death, Jesus says that the ruler of this world is coming, but that he has no power over him; and in 16.11, we learn that Jesus' 'going-away' means that the ruler of this world is judged.

The death of Jesus is seen as an eschatological battle, in which Jesus triumphs over evil.

The story of the anointing of Jesus (12.1–8) is very similar to the one we have in Mark. In John, however, the woman (here identified as Mary, sister of Lazarus), anoints the feet, not the head of Jesus, so that her action is not seen as a 'coronation'; nor do we have the comment which links it with Jesus' burial. Nevertheless, the story still points forward to Jesus' death, for the criticism of the woman's action, voiced here by Judas, is answered by Jesus' comment that 'You have the poor with you always; but you do not always have me.'

Next in John comes the triumphal entry into Jerusalem (12.12–19), and in this gospel it is indeed a real triumph. Whereas in Mark, Jesus is simply hailed by fellow pilgrims as one who comes 'in the name of the Lord', in John, the crowd sets out to meet Jesus and welcomes him to Jerusalem with palm branches and acclamations; their cries spell out what is only hinted at in Mark and clearly identify him as 'the king of Israel'. John also tells us plainly something else that is only hinted at in Mark – namely, that Jesus' entry into Jerusalem on the back of a young ass fulfilled the words in Zechariah about the arrival of Zion's king. His arrival is seen as a royal progress – and yet, says John, 'his disciples did not understand these things at first, and realized their significance only after Jesus had been glorified': John is telling his story with the benefit of hindsight and is anxious that we his readers should see what was hidden at the time.

John's account of Jesus' last meal with his disciples is strikingly different from that given us by the Synoptics; nevertheless he performs symbolic actions and speaks about service and about the meaning of his death and departure. Instead of bread and wine, he takes a basin and a towel (13.1–11). The actions he performs are quite different from those in the Synoptics, yet they express the same truth, that he lives – and dies – for others. The meaning of what he does is obscure to the disciples, but once again, as so often in John, we are told that they will understand 'later' – which now can only mean after Jesus' death. In this way, his washing of their feet is linked with his death, which is thus seen to be an act of service. What Jesus does for them symbolizes first of all the fact that they have 'a part with' him: the language reminds us of other passages which speak of the close relationship between Jesus and his followers – of the Johannine description of the vine and its branches in

John 15 and the Pauline image of Christians as members of the body of Christ;[11] it reminds us, too, of the synoptic account of the Last Supper where, in distributing the bread, Jesus shares his 'body', himself, with his disciples. The washing signifies also that they are clean – a link this time with Matthew's account of the Last Supper, where Jesus' blood is said to be poured out 'for the forgiveness of sins' (26.28). But the service Jesus performs for the disciples is also one that they ought to perform for one another (v. 14). This is one of the echoes which we occasionally find in John of the theme which was so prominent in Mark, that the disciples must follow the example of their Lord. We have another in John 12.25f., in a saying reminiscent of Mark 8.35: 'He who loves his life loses it, and he who hates his life in this world will keep it for eternal life. If any one serves me, he must follow me.' As in Mark, the disciples claim to be able to face up to this challenge: in John 11.16, they recognize the danger involved in Jesus going into Judaea when Thomas says 'Let us go too, so that we may die with him'. And in the Farewell Discourses, John's equivalent of Mark's so-called 'Apocalyptic Discourse' (Mark 13), Jesus warns the disciples that they will be hated as he has been hated, that they will be persecuted, excommunicated from the synagogues, and killed (John 15.18–21; 16.1–4). But all that lies in the future: in 13.36–38 he warns Peter that he will deny him that same night; like the revelation in 13.18–26 that one of the twelve will betray him, this section is very similar at this point to the synoptic account of the Last Supper (Mark 14.17–21, 26–31 and parallels).

Although the Johannine account of Jesus' last meal with his disciples is so very different from that in the synoptic gospels, therefore, there are fascinating parallels with the synoptic tradition. Nevertheless, one of the enigmas of the Fourth Gospel is why it is that John does not record the tradition about the bread and wine at this point in his story, since it is not only the Synoptics, but Paul as well, who record that it was 'on the night that Jesus was handed-over' that he took bread and took a cup. But John does include his own tradition about the body and blood of Jesus earlier in his narrative, in chapter 6, and it is characteristic of John that he should draw our attention to the significance of Jesus and his actions from the very beginning of the story. Jesus was recognized as Messiah by his disciples at their very first

---

11 Romans 12; 1 Corinthians 12.

meeting, singled-out as the one who takes away sin by John the Baptist; already he has 'manifested his glory' (the glory that belongs to the cross) in Cana of Galilee, and spoken about his death and resurrection in the temple at Jerusalem (at the feast of Passover); already in Jesus' discourses we have had spelt out for us the significance of his coming and of his words and deeds; already the Jews have tried to kill him (5.16–18). We know the outcome of the story from the beginning – and we know its significance, because John has woven into the story the interpretation which Christians have given to it in the light of subsequent events. So it is perhaps not surprising that he gives such prominence to the stories of Jesus providing wine (2.1–10)[12] and bread (6.1–15, 25–65), or that he includes eucharistic sayings in the second of these: for those with eyes to see, both stories point to Jesus' death and resurrection, since Jesus reveals his glory in the first, and the second takes place when Passover was near.

The sayings in John 6 come at the end of a discourse about Jesus as the bread of life which follows the miracle of the feeding of the crowd. The passage takes the form of a 'midrash' – an exposition of Jewish scripture: the bread which is given from heaven, spoken of in Exodus 16, is not, as had hitherto been supposed, the manna eaten by the Israelites in the wilderness, but Christ himself, who is the true bread, to which the manna points forward. Now manna was often understood as a symbol for the law, which was also given to the people 'through Moses', and John emphasizes throughout his gospel that the law points forward to Jesus. So both the manna and the law find their fulfilment or completion in Christ. The law revealed the will of God to Israel, but now God is more fully revealed to his people in the person of Jesus; John has said something very similar already in the prologue: the law was given through Moses, but grace and truth came in Jesus Christ.

God is revealed in the words and deeds of Jesus, but he is revealed supremely in his death. The bread which God gives is Jesus (6.32), and the bread which Jesus gives is his flesh (6.51). The final paragraph of the discourse is one of the most difficult in the whole gospel: Jesus demands that his disciples eat his flesh and drink his blood, for only so can

---

12 This story may well be based on the tradition recorded in Mark 2.19–20, 22.

they have eternal life. John does here what neither Paul nor the other evangelists do – speaks about eating flesh and drinking blood. No Jew could have contemplated for one moment eating human flesh or drinking any kind of blood; the blood was always carefully drained from meat, lest any of it should be eaten, because the life was in the blood. Of course the words of Jesus are said to have offended the Jews! Their very absurdity provides the clue to their meaning: here, as so often in John's gospel, Jesus is talking at one level – the spiritual level – while everyone else is plodding along with their feet firmly on the ground, taking everything literally. But we cannot take the words literally. We may compare his words to Nicodemus about being born again (3.3–8): the Greek word *anōthen* is in fact ambiguous – it can mean 'a second time', but it can also mean 'from above'; Nicodemus scoffs at the notion of entering again into the womb, but Jesus is talking about entering the kingdom of heaven. Again, we remember how in his conversation with the Samaritan woman, Jesus offers her living water, but she can think only of the daily trek to the well (4.10–15). The problem as John sees it is summed up in 8.23, where Jesus says: You are from below, I am from above; you are of this world, I am not of this world'. His words about flesh and blood must, of course, be understood in the same way: those who believe in him are totally dependent on him; they participate in him, share his life. Jesus gives his flesh and blood by his death, and it is through his death that believers find life. The 'offence' caused by Jesus' words here is also symbolic, for it reminds us of the offence caused by a gospel about a crucified saviour.

John has chosen to spell out this eucharistic teaching in chapter 6, and to focus his account of Jesus' last meal on his action in washing the disciples' feet and on the Farewell Discourses, in which he spells out the ongoing relationship between Jesus and his followers and the need for them to continue his work. In John's narrative, the account of the arrest follows immediately after Jesus and his disciples arrive in the garden after supper (18.1–11). John tells the story in such a way as to emphasize that Jesus is in control: Jesus, he tells us, knows everything that is to befall him (v. 4), and insists that he must drink the cup which the Father has given him (v. 11) – another echo of the Gethsemane story, but how different it sounds when it is reported in this way, for there is not a moment's hesitation. From the minute that his enemies arrive, Jesus takes the initiative: he comes forward, asks the questions, and even issues the commands. And when he identifies himself with the words 'I am he', which echo the divine name, the soldiers are so overcome that they fall backwards on the ground. Even his arrest seems to be part of a royal progress.

John reports a trial scene before Annas, whom he describes as father-in-law of the high priest Caiaphas (18.12–23), but tells us nothing about what happened when Jesus is sent on to Caiaphas himself.[13] The account of Jesus' interrogation by Annas is sandwiched between the story of Peter's three-fold denial, and the irony of the situation is brought out by John in his own unique way through his arrangement of the material. First, Peter is asked whether he is not one of Jesus' disciples, and he declares that he is not. Then Jesus is questioned about his disciples and about his teaching; he says nothing about his disciples (perhaps because it was useless to appeal to them!), but concerning his teaching, he tells his questioners to consult those who heard him. Finally the scene switches back to the courtyard, where Peter is asked again whether he is not a disciple, and whether he was not in the garden with Jesus, and he twice more denies any knowledge of Jesus. As in the Synoptics, the picture of Jesus, firm under interrogation (though the questions put to him are different here), stands in contrast with that of Peter, who denies every suggestion that he is a disciple. The scene now moves quickly to the residence of the Roman governor. Notice the irony in John's comment that the 'Jews did not enter the praetorium 'so that they might not be defiled, but might eat the Passover' (18.28): in spite of their precautions they are of course defiling themselves by engineering the death of the true Passover lamb. Notice, too, how the fact that the Jews hand Jesus over to Pilate for execution, and refuse to judge him themselves, is understood by John as a fulfilment of Jesus' prophecy concerning the manner in which he was to die: what takes place is now seen not simply as the fulfilment of scripture, but as the fulfilment of Jesus' own words (18.29–32), because his will is identified with that of his Father. Once again, we have the impression that Jesus is in total command of everything that is taking place. In a series of conversations, Pilate makes repeated attempts to release

---

13 John's account is somewhat confused. He appears to describe Annas himself as high priest in v. 19. The Synoptics do not mention an interrogation by Annas.

Jesus, since he realizes that Jesus is innocent of the charges brought against him, but he is powerless to resist. One might perhaps think that it is the powers of darkness that are in control and that have swamped both Jesus and Pilate, preventing the latter's attempts to uphold what is right. But no! The power which Pilate exercises over Jesus has been given him from above (19.11), and the drama which is being enacted has been written by God. We remember the words of 14.30f: 'the ruler of this world has no power over me; but I do as the Father has commanded me.'

But the rule of Jesus belongs to another world. In answer to Pilate's question, 'Are you the king of the Jews?' Jesus replies, 'My kingship is not of this world' (18.36). Once again, we have a conversation on two levels: Pilate can think only in this-worldly terms and is bewildered by Jesus' words. He insists on calling Jesus 'king of the Jews' and his soldiers mock him, crowning him with thorns and clothing him in purple and hailing him as king (19.1–3). Pilate presents Jesus to the people with the words 'Here is your king!' (19.14) and insists that the inscription on the cross reads 'the king of the Jews' (19.19–22). The inscription is written in three languages, in order that the whole world may know the truth. As in Mark, Jesus is proclaimed as king on the cross – but his kingship is denied by the Jews, who protest at what Pilate has written. In rejecting their king and claiming that they have no king but Caesar they commit the ultimate blasphemy. The cry we might expect to hear from Jews is 'We have no king but *God* – and his vicegerent, his Messiah'. So Pilate finally hands Jesus over to them to be crucified: the verb, of course, is *paradidōmi*.[14]

The account of the crucifixion itself is quite different in atmosphere from the story told in Mark. Instead of the horror – the taunts, the cry of dereliction, the darkness – we have a scene of calm. Even here, Jesus seems to be still majestic, in control of what is happening. John tells us that Jesus goes out, bearing his own cross (19.17), whereas in the Synoptics, Simon of Cyrene is compelled to carry it. Some commentators explain John's omission of this tradition as deliberately anti-Docetic; he wants to avoid any possibility of it being suggested that it was Simon, not Jesus, who was crucified. Others suggest that John is thinking of the story of Isaac in Genesis 22, carrying wood for his own sacrifice on his back. Yet another suggestion links it with the saying in

14 19.16. See also 18.30, 36; 19.11.

Luke 14.27 – 'Whoever does not bear his own cross and come after me, cannot be my disciple'.[15] Has John perhaps deliberately worded his account with that saying in mind? Whether he has or not, those who are familiar with it will recognize that in bearing his own cross Jesus does what he challenges his followers to do. But perhaps the simplest explanation for John's wording is that he simply wishes to stress that Jesus is deliberately laying down his life: even at this point, he is doing what he has come to do, and is not being compelled. And of course, what happens is the fulfilment of scripture: four times in the course of the crucifixion narrative – in 19.24, 28, 36 and 37 – John uses fulfilment formulae, followed by Old Testament quotations. Whatever took place happened in order that the scripture might be fulfilled. Similar formulae are found earlier, referring to the passion, at 13.18 and 15.25. These references to scripture are much more explicit than in the Synoptics, which suggests that John was concerned to spell out the way in which everything that happened took place in accordance with scripture.

John adds the story of Jesus' words to his mother and to the beloved disciple (19.25–27), and once again we find Jesus in control of the situation. Even when he says 'I thirst' it was 'to fulfil the scripture'; John certainly seems here to be interpreting what we would normally think of as 'result' in terms of 'purpose'. Jesus' thirst is the closest we come to the agony which we have in Mark, and the end of the story is very different from Mark's. Jesus' final words are 'It is finished' – a cry of triumph (19.30): Jesus has completed the work which he came to do.

Verses 31–7 describe how Jesus' bones are not broken, but his side is pierced. Both things are seen as the fulfilment of scripture – but what scripture is being quoted in v. 36? It might be Ps. 34.20, but almost certainly there is a reference here to Ex. 12.46 or Num. 9.12, where instructions are given about the Passover lamb. If Jesus dies as the true Passover lamb, then his bones must not be broken. This perhaps provides a clue as to how we are to interpret the water and the blood, which flow from Jesus' side when it is pierced with a lance. What do these signify? Some commentators suggest that they stand for the sacraments, but it would be odd to find the eucharist represented by blood

---

15 C. H. Dodd, *Historical Tradition in the Fourth Gospel*, Cambridge 1963, pp. 124f.

alone, though of course the blood flows from the body of Jesus. Others suggest that the blood and water are guarantees of the reality of Jesus' death, and that may be part of the explanation (v. 35). But John is certainly likely to have seen symbolic meaning in them. Perhaps they stand for the water and blood of birth, and so symbolize the new birth of those who are born *anōthen* (John 3). If Jesus died as the true Passover lamb, then perhaps the pouring out of the blood is a natural corollary, for the blood of the sacrifice has to be poured out. As for the water, in John 7.37–9 Jesus is said to have summoned those who were thirsty to come to him and drink. His summons is followed by an obscure and unknown quotation about water flowing from someone's belly, which is then interpreted of the Spirit, which is to be given when Jesus is glorified. So perhaps the water which flows from Jesus' side points forward to the gift of the Spirit, which takes place in 20.22. Once again, we do not necessarily have to choose between these explanations, for John may have had more than one meaning in mind. Whatever the true interpretation, it looks as if he understands blood and water as symbolizing in some way the new life which comes out of Jesus' death. Certainly we have, earlier in the Gospel, sayings about drinking both the water and the blood which Jesus provides (4.10–15; 6.53–6). The final paradox is that they are supplied by the one who thirsts on the cross.

Even though at a superficial level John's account of what took place on Good Friday is similar to what the Synoptics tell us, the effect of John's passion narrative is very different from theirs. Indeed, there is a sense in which John does not contain a 'passion' narrative, and it might be truer to describe his account as a 'glory' narrative, for it is the story of how Jesus was glorified and how he glorified God through his death. John has already provided us with the key to understanding the story in the verb *doxazō*.[16] In this sense, John's account of the crucifixion is far removed from that of Mark. Whereas Mark tells the story of Jesus' suffering on the cross, feeling utterly cut off from God, John tells the story of Jesus triumphant on the cross, at one with God. Which of them is right? The answer must be both! The paradox of the cross is that God is found, and revealed, in the midst of suffering and pain. Paul knew this, and used both ideas: he sees the cross as the sign that Christ was under the curse, that he became sin, that he knew the

16 See above, n. 3.

darkness of isolation from God;[17] and yet he sees it also as the glorious demonstration of the wisdom and strength of God.[18] For both Paul and John, the cross is seen in the light of the triumphant resurrection which followed. We need both Mark's story and John's – Mark's to remind us of the cost, John's to assure us of the glory. Each of the evangelists has something to add to our understanding of the death of Jesus; even when we have read them all, we have only begun to explore a mystery whose significance can never be exhausted.

'The cross is seen in the light of the triumphant resurrection which followed' – and in spite of John's understanding of the cross as itself an exaltation, the resurrection is still a necessary part of the story. John tells the resurrection stories in such a way as to remind us of the importance of faith. As in all the gospels, the first visit to the tomb on Easter Sunday was made by a woman – in John, by one woman only, namely Mary Magdala. She reported to the disciples that the tomb was empty, and Peter and the 'beloved' disciple rushed to see for themselves. Peter burst into the tomb and saw that it was empty, apart from the graveclothes – in other words, he saw the evidence – but the beloved disciple 'saw and believed' (20.1–8).

Mary now sees two angels, but the news that Jesus has been raised is conveyed to her by Jesus himself: if the synoptic story is remarkable in that there the only witnesses to the empty tomb and the first people to hear the news of Jesus' resurrection were women, John's account is equally remarkable in that a woman is the first person to see the Risen Lord (20.10–18). It is later in the day that he appears to ten of the disciples (20.19–23), and a week later that he appears again to the same group with the addition of Thomas (20.24–9); the story of 'Doubting Thomas', who had been absent on the first occasion and who refused to believe until he saw the Lord for himself, stands in contrast to that of the beloved disciple, and points us to the fact that stories about an empty tomb and about appearances of the Risen Lord are not in themselves sufficient to bring men and women to Christian faith. Thomas demands more – and he is given what he demands – but the story is used to remind us that true faith does not depend on seeing and touching.

John's account comes to an obvious conclusion at the end

---

17 Gal. 3.13; 2 Cor. 5.21.
18 I Cor. 1.18–31.

of chapter 20, and most commentators believe that the gospel originally ended at this point. Someone has added another section however – chapter 21 – telling the story of Jesus' appearance to his disciples when they were fishing on the lake of Galilee. Jesus enables the disciples to make a huge catch of fish, and prepares a fire; then he offers them bread and fish: the Risen Lord thus provides sustenance to his followers (21.1–14). He also offers forgiveness to Simon, with the threefold question 'Do you love me?' and with the commission to tend his flock (21.15–19). In the final challenge, 'Follow me,' the man who had denied that he was a disciple is given the opportunity to begin again on the path of discipleship – and warned that following will mean that he, like Jesus, will glorify God through martyrdom. The chapter may be an addition to the gospel, but it certainly provides an appropriate ending.

CHAPTER SEVEN

Hebrews

The Epistle to the Hebrews[1] is dominated by the theme of the death of Christ. It is the most sustained piece of writing on the subject in the New Testament – there is only one chapter (11) where it is not mentioned – and it will therefore be necessary for us to try to follow the argument fairly closely.

The author's exploration of the theme is set in the context of his affirmation of the superiority of Christ to everything that has preceded him. This underlying conviction is summed up in the opening verses of the epistle, which establish Christ's superiority to all past revelation:

'In times past, God spoke in many and in various ways to our forefathers through the prophets, but in these final days he has spoken to us through a Son, whom he appointed the heir of all things and through whom he created the universe. He is the radiance of his glory and the stamp of his very being, upholding the universe by his word of power' (1.1–3a).

The ideas expressed here are familiar from other parts of the New Testament,[2] but Hebrews moves immediately to a statement of the main theme of the epistle:

'When he had brought about the purification from sins, he

---

1 The book is described as an 'epistle' on the basis of the greetings at the end, but it lacks the opening formula common in letters of the time; it is possible that it is a homily that has been adapted for use as a letter. The term 'Hebrews' reflects the traditional view that it was addressed to Jewish Christians tempted to relapse into Judaism, but this is by no means certain, though it seems probable that the author was a Jewish Christian. No one knows who he was, where or when he wrote, to whom he was writing or the circumstances that led him to write: we can only try to deduce these things from the 'letter' itself.

2 In particular Col. 1.15–17 and John 1.1–18. The language echoes passages describing the role of wisdom or Torah (the law) in God's purpose, e.g. Prov. 3.19; 8.22–31; Wisdom 7.25–8.1; 9.1–6; Sirach 24.

sat down at the right hand of majesty on high, having become as much superior to the angels as the name he has inherited is more excellent than theirs' (1.3b–4).

Christ's superiority goes back to the beginning of time, but it was nevertheless established through his death and exaltation, and that death is interpreted in particular as a means of bringing about the purification from sins.

Christ's superiority to all things is then explored in three different ways. First, he is superior to angels, since he alone is God's Son, invited to sit at God's right hand; evidence for this is supplied by various proof-texts (1.5–14). At this point the author pauses to remind his readers that, since the message they have received is so much greater than the revelation (i.e. the law) received in the past through angels, they must be careful not to forsake it, lest they incur penalties even greater than those which came to transgressors of the law (2.1–4). Returning to his main argument regarding the superiority of Christ to the angels, he maintains once again that this superiority is established *through Christ's death and resurrection*. In a remarkable exposition of Psalm 8, the author argues that the passage about the man/son of man who is made lower than the angels and then crowned with glory and honour has been fulfilled in the case of Jesus, who is crowned because he suffered death (2.5–9). He then explores the significance of this for men and women: in order that God might bring them to glory, as his children, it was necessary for Christ, the 'pioneer' of their salvation, to be 'made perfect' through suffering (2.10). He is the one who sanctifies and they are the sanctified, but they have one origin, and he is their brother; he shared in their flesh and blood in order that through his death he might destroy the devil, who had the power of death, and set free those whom the devil had enslaved (2.11–15). Since it was men and women whom Christ was helping it was necessary for him to become like them in everything, in order that he might become a merciful high priest in God's service, making atonement for the sins of the people (2.16–17). Because he himself has been tested by suffering, he is now able to help those who are in the process of being tested (2.18).

Throughout this section the author insists very firmly on Christ's full humanity: it is only someone who is 'one of us' who can be our high priest. It was necessary for Christ to share human suffering in order to bring men and women to glory, necessary for him to share our flesh and blood in order to free us from the fear of death, necessary for him to experience testing or temptation in order to offer expiation for sins. The assumptions here are very similar to those significant statements of Paul's in which he declares that Christ became what we are, in order that we might become what he is.[3] As our author puts it – the Son of God was made for a while lower than the angels, one with men and women in suffering and death, weakness and temptation, in order that he might enable men and women to become 'sons' of God and be crowned with the same glory.[4] But woven into this, we see another indication of the distinctive way in which the author of Hebrews works out this theme – the notion of Christ as the perfect high priest who can achieve the purification from sin.

Christ's superiority is now worked out in relation to Moses. We have to remember that for the Jews, Moses was the greatest figure of all times, and the notion that anyone was superior to him was almost blasphemous. Jesus our high priest was faithful, just as Moses had been – yet Jesus is worthy of far more glory than Moses, in the same way that the builder of a house[5] is more worthy of honour than the house itself (3.1–3). But the builder of all things is God himself (3.4); the comment seems hardly relevant[6] – except that it suggests that if Jesus himself is seen as a builder, he is once again being thought of as the agent through whom God

---

3 See above, chapter 2.

4 There is another possible parallel in this section to an idea found in Paul as well as in Mark/Matthew. Most of our mss tell us in v. 9 that Christ died *chariti Theou*, 'by the grace of God', but according to many of the Fathers the original text said that he died *chōris Theou*, 'without God'. Some commentators prefer the latter reading on the principle that it is more difficult and therefore more likely to have been the original reading, which has been changed to something more comprehensible. The former reading is much better attested, however, and it is possible to interpret *chōris Theou* as a gloss explaining v. 8 ('everything was subjected to Christ except God himself') which found its way into the text; accordingly, most editors and translators assume that *chariti Theou* is the original reading. If we adopt the alternative reading as the original one, however, the statement would prove to be a very interesting parallel to the cry of dereliction in Mark 15.34/Matt. 27.46, and to Paul's identification of Christ with the curse of God and with sin in Gal. 3.13 and 2 Cor. 5.21.

5 It is possible to translate the Greek here as 'the founder of a household' rather than 'the builder of a house'. By the time we reach v. 6b, the author is certainly thinking of a community rather than a building.

6 It is often treated by commentators as a parenthesis.

creates the universe. And so he is, for Moses, we are told, 'was faithful in God's whole household as a servant', but Christ is faithful '*as a son* [i.e. sharing his Father's characteristics] *over* the household'; and now we learn that we (i.e. Christian believers) are the members of that household (3.5–6).

As in the previous section (in 2.1–4), the author now warns his readers that they must not fail, but this time his warning is an extended one (3.7–4.13). They must not be rebellious, as their forefathers had been; they can be encouraged, because they have become partners with Christ (3.14), and because the promise of a 'sabbath rest' still awaits the people of God (4.9). And so the author returns yet again to his main theme: 'since we have a great high priest who has passed through the heavens – Jesus, the Son of God – let us hold fast to the faith we profess. For we do not have a high priest who is unable to sympathize with our weaknesses, but we have one who has been tested in every way as we are, only without sinning. Let us therefore boldly approach the throne of grace, in order that we may receive mercy and find grace to help in time of need' (4.14–16).

And now our author begins to explore this theme of Christ's high-priesthood, as he spells out the superiority of Christ to all human high priests. They have sympathy with their fellows because they too are weak and have to make sin-offerings for themselves as well as for the people. None of them arrogates the honour of high-priesthood to himself, since each has to be called by God – and so it is with Christ, even though he was not a descendant of Aaron, as were all other high priests, but was appointed according to the order of Melchizedek (5.1–6). The next few verses are apparently intended to demonstrate that Jesus is no less able to sympathise with the weak than are other high priests, because 'in the course of his earthly life he offered up prayers and petitions with loud cries and tears to the one who was able to save him from death . . . . Although he was a son, he learned obedience through what he suffered' (5.7–8). This is an idea we have met already in 2.18.

If we are finding the author's train of thought hard to follow, we may be encouraged by the fact that at this point in the argument he pauses to comment that his teaching is probably too difficult for his readers to comprehend! Others before us have struggled with his message. The reason for his doubts, however, seems to be what he considers to be the obtuseness of his readers rather than the obscurity of his own teaching. Those whom he is addressing have apparently proved themselves somewhat slow to learn (5.11–14). He warns them once more of the danger of falling away from the truth they have seen and received, and picks up his main theme again in the final verse of chapter 6: Jesus has entered the sanctuary behind the curtain as a forerunner on our behalf, having become a high priest for ever according to the order of Melchizedek.

The mysterious figure of Melchizedek is now explained. Most modern readers are somewhat puzzled by Melchizedek, about whom so little is known, but who is clearly so important to our author. Recent discoveries at Qumran have revealed that Melchizedek was an important figure in at least one of the writings known to the community there – and possibly to other Jews of the first century A.D. – rather as Enoch, who also appears only briefly in the Old Testament, became a central figure in later Jewish writings.[7] It may well be, therefore, that Melchizedek would have been a familiar figure to the epistle's first readers, and that they would not have been at all puzzled by the important role he plays in the argument. From the story in Gen. 14.18–20, our author deduces that, since Melchizedek blessed Abraham and received tithes from him, he must have been greater than Abraham, greater also than Abraham's descendant Levi (7.1–10). The figure of Melchizedek enables the author to explain how Jesus could be a high priest when he was a member of the tribe of Judah and not the tribe of Levi, to which the Jewish priests belonged (7.12–14). But it also enables him to argue that the levitical priesthood was imperfect, since if it had fulfilled its purpose there would have been no need for another kind of priest (7.11). This new priest is of course Jesus, who has been declared by God to be 'a priest for ever, according to the order of Melchizedek' (7.17, quoting Ps. 110.4): Jesus owes his priesthood to 'the power of a life that cannot be destroyed', and not to rules of physical descent (7.15f.), and thus, like Melchizedek, 'remains a priest for ever' (7.3). His appointment means that the old system of sacrifices is abolished as ineffectual

---

7 The Qumran material about Melchizedek is found in 11Q Melch. Melchizedek appears also in 2 Enoch 71–2, the date of which is uncertain – possibly the late first century A.D.

(7.15–19). His superiority is seen in the fact that God himself has guaranteed the efficacy of his priesthood by swearing an oath in appointing him, and in the fact that this priesthood is permanent, and is not terminated by death, so that he is able to save men and women completely (7.20–25). It is seen also in his holiness, which sets him apart from sinners (so that he has no need to offer sacrifices for himself, as does the Jewish high priest), and in the fact that the offering he made was 'once for all', and not a daily sacrifice (7.26–28).[8]

This new high priest has taken his seat at the right hand of God, a minister in the true sanctuary in heaven, of which the earthly sanctuary is only a shadowy copy (8.1–5). Jesus is the mediator of a better covenant than the one made with Moses – it is the new covenant spoken of by Jeremiah, which makes the old one obsolete (8.6–13). The first covenant had regulations for worship in an earthly temple: its inner sanctuary is the Holy of Holies, into which the high priest alone enters once a year, but the sacrifices he offers are of limited value, since they deal only with external cleansing in this present age (9.1–10). But Christ is the high priest of a heavenly temple, and the sacrifice he offered was his own blood, not that of goats and calves, so that he has entered the sanctuary once for all, and secured an eternal redemption (9.11–12). If the blood of goats and bulls can cleanse men and women from outward impurity, how much greater is the power of Christ's blood, which can cleanse our consciences (9.13–14).

In the next section, our author plays on the double meaning of the Greek word diathēkē, which can mean both 'covenant' and 'will'. A will can be ratified only when a death has occurred – and the covenant of which he is speaking also requires a death, in this case that of Christ. The same was true of the old covenant – indeed, he concludes, 'one might almost say that under the law it is by blood that everything is cleansed, and without the shedding of blood there is no forgiveness' (9.15–22). The author here sets out the assumptions underlying the Old Testament accounts of the covenant and the cult: a covenant could be ratified only through a sacrificial death; forgiveness was possible only if blood was shed. But it has to be remembered that there were plenty of Jews who experienced God's

---

8 In fact the high priest did not offer sacrifice daily; the author seems to be thinking here of the daily sacrifices offered by the priests in general.

forgiveness in other ways:[9] it would be foolish to assume, on the basis of this remark, that God 'could not' forgive sins unless Christ had died.[10]

But our author is arguing on the basis of the sacrificial system, according to which sacrifice was the only means of purification. The provisions of the cult thus provide him with an *explanation* of Christ's death: his death was both a ratification of a better covenant and a means of expiation. For if the blood of goats and bulls can remove defilement from the flesh, the superior sacrifice of the blood of Christ can certainly purify our consciences (9.13f.).

The contrast is now drawn between the sacrifices made in the temple, which is a copy of the heavenly one, and the sacrifice of Christ, who has entered a sanctuary not made with human hands – i.e. heaven itself. Instead of the sacrifice offered every year by the Levitical high priest, we have a sacrifice made once for all. But Christ is victim as well as high priest, and he was offered 'to bear the sins of many' – an echo of Isa. 53.12. As elsewhere 'many' is not an exclusive term (the *REB* has tried to convey this by the translation 'mankind' – which is also not intended to be an exclusive term!); the verb 'bear' (*anapherō*) can be used as a technical term for offering sacrifices, and the sense in this context seems to be that Christ was offered up as a sacrifice to deal with sins, as was the sin-offering sacrificed by the high priest on the Day of Atonement, which purified the sanctuary and cleansed the people from their sins (9.23–8).

So the law contains but a shadow of the good things to come: its repeated sacrifices cannot bring perfection – if they did, they would not need to be repeated (10.1–4). These sacrifices are not pleasing to God, but that made by Christ is, because it is a sacrifice of the will and demonstrates his total obedience to God (10.5–10). Moreover, his self-offering is the means by which we are sanctified (10.10).

---

9 There are in the Old Testament plenty of prayers for forgiveness and assurances that God forgives sins which make no reference to sacrifice: e.g. 1 Kgs. 8.30; Pss. 25.18; 32.1f.; 85.2f.; 86.5; 103.3; 130.3f.; Isa. 1.18; 33.24; Amos 7.2f. In the Qumran literature, see 1QS 11; 1QH 1 and 6.
10 Jesus is said to have offered forgiveness during his ministy. E.g. Mark 2.5; Luke 7.37f.; 19.9f. Cf. also Matt. 6.12; Luke 6.37.

And now our author contrasts the daily sacrifices offered by the priests with the once-for-all offering 'for sins' made by Christ, which has a permanent effect; his work completed, he has now sat down at God's right hand (10.11–18).

The next section introduces a new idea: because of Christ's self-offering, Christians have confidence to enter the sanctuary, for he has opened up a new and living way for them through the curtain – that is, his flesh. This final phrase puzzles commentators, who give various explanations of its meaning,[11] but the most likely is that it reflects the tradition that the curtain was torn in two at the moment of Jesus' death, thus opening up the way into the inner shrine. In the earthly temple, only the high priest could enter the sanctuary through the curtain, but now Christians are able to enter the Holy of Holies! Those who enter must be clean – washed with pure water, like the priests of old, and with their consciences cleansed (10.19–22).

And now our author turns to admonition once again – and as before, he reminds his readers of what happened to those who failed in the past: if judgement fell on those who transgressed the law, how much worse will be the fate of those who spurn the Son of God (10.23–31). They must remember their past devotion and continue in faith (10.32–9).

This is really the end of the author's exposition of the meaning of Christ's death, though after his eulogy of faith in chapter 11 he continues his exhortation, and the death of Christ is never far from his thoughts. Thus he urges Christians to run the race before them with perseverance – as did Jesus, the pioneer and perfecter of their faith, who for the sake of the joy set before him endured the cross, despising its shame, and has now sat down at God's right hand. Christ's endurance of hostility must be an example to them in their struggles (12.1–4). Later in the chapter, describing the superiority of the revelation granted to Christians over that given to their Jewish forefathers on Sinai (12.18–24), he speaks of Jesus as the mediator of a new covenant, whose sprinkled blood has better things to say than that of Abel (since that cried out for vengeance, not forgiveness, Gen. 4.10).

---

11 Some (e.g. Westcott and Montefiore) suggest that it is meant to explain 'the way', but most take it as defining the veil.

The imagery of the Day of Atonement is picked up in chapter 13: the bodies of the animals killed as a sin-offering were burnt outside the camp, and in a similar way Jesus suffered outside the gate of Jerusalem. Christians, too, must be prepared to join him 'outside the camp', bearing the same disgrace (13.10–13). The final benediction describes God as the one who brought our Lord Jesus back from the dead, by the blood of an eternal covenant. The words 'by the blood of a covenant' echo Zech. 9.11, where they refer to the grounds on which God rescues the people of Judah. The thought here seems to be that the resurrection of Jesus is itself the result of the covenant made in his blood; and if he, the great shepherd has been raised, he will take care of his sheep (13.20–21).

* * *

Why did the author of Hebrews compose this extended argument about the superiority of the work of Christ to the cult? No-one can be sure, though the traditional explanation is that his readers were Jewish Christians who were 'lapsing back' into Judaism. But if Acts[12] is to be believed, then the first generation of Christians at least saw no incompatibility between worship in the temple and their Christian faith. Perhaps by the time our author was writing, tensions had arisen: if, for example, his community was a mixed Jewish-Gentile Christian one, in which those who were Jewish by birth continued to send offerings to the temple while those who were Gentile felt no such loyalty, he may have felt that it was necessary to sever all connection with the temple; but if so, there is no indication of any tension between Jew and Gentile in the letter. Perhaps there was hostility between the Jewish Christian community and their fellow Jews; but again, there is no sign of this in the letter – unless it is in the hints of persecution in 12.3f and 13.12f. Or perhaps he was writing after A.D.70, when the temple had been destroyed, and was concerned to comfort his readers by assuring them that the temple was no longer needed; but if so, it is strange that there is no reference in the letter to the temple's destruction. Whatever the explanation for our author developing his argument, there is no reason to believe that Jewish worshippers felt the dissatisfaction with the cult that he expresses. He argues *backwards*, from the salvation he has experienced through Christ, to the inadequacies of every-

12 Acts 2.46; 3.1–10; 20.16.

thing that went before – much as Paul argued backwards from the work of Christ to the inadequacies of the Law.[13] Only those who have enjoyed the luxury of electric light realize the shortcomings of a box of candles: the one gives permanent bright illumination, the other, weak, guttering lights that have to be constantly replaced because their power is exhausted. Such is the contrast, for our author, between the perfect sacrifice offered by Christ 'once and for all' (7.27; 9.12; 10.10) and the endlessly repeated offerings of the Jewish sacrificial system.

Yet however feeble it may be, a candle does give light: in the same way, the Jewish sacrificial system is understood by our author to be a copy of the heavenly reality (8.5; 9.23). Commentators have often assumed that he was influenced here by Platonic ideas of reality, which interpreted everything in the visible world as a 'shadow' or copy of a heavenly original. Plato's ideas certainly influenced the first-century Jewish writer Philo, but there is no need to assume Platonic influence here. Firstly, because the argument in Hebrews is based on Ex. 25.40 (quoted in Heb. 8.5), where Moses is instructed to make the sanctuary in accordance with the design revealed to him on Sinai: the author thus has scriptural justification for his idea that the temple is a copy of a heavenly original – the innovative step is to link this with Christ. Secondly, because the idea that events on earth take place in accordance with a pattern laid down in heaven is a common one in Jewish apocalyptic writing. To be sure, the hope expressed in apocalyptic is that what now is in heaven will one day be effected on earth, whereas in Hebrews, Christ's entry into heaven is the culmination of the sacrifices offered by the high priests, which are thereby rendered unnecessary. But the 'true' sanctuary is heaven (9.24), which exists from all eternity – which is, indeed, outside time – and the idea that what 'takes place' there is vital for the well-being of men and women would be a familiar one to Jewish readers of the first century A.D. In Christ's death and ascension, the eternal has impinged upon the temporal: this is why it is 'once for all', and why there is no need for further sacrifices. The old cult is obsolete and the temple defunct, because not Christ only but his followers also have entered into the Holy of Holies.

---

13 Cf. E. P. Sanders, *Paul and Palestinian Judaism*, London 1977, pp. 442–7.

It is vital to his argument, moreover, that the scriptures show knowledge of 'something better', now fulfilled in Christ. Scripture tells us about the heavenly sanctuary (Heb. 8.5, quoting Ex. 25.40), and about the better covenant, of which Jesus is the mediator (Heb. 8.6–13, quoting Jer. 31.31–4). Scripture knows about a better priesthood (Heb. 7.1–28, quoting Gen. 14.17–20 and Ps. 110.4) and about a better sacrifice (Heb. 10.1–10, quoting Ps. 40.6–8). This appeal to the witness of scripture is very similar to that made by Paul, when he argues that scripture points beyond the provisions of the Law to something greater, which thus makes the provisions themselves obsolete.

We have seen that for our author *what* Christ *does* depends very clearly on *who* he *is*. He is Son of God, superior to the angels, greater than Moses, a better high priest than the descendants of Levi. But equally important is his identity with humanity and his obedience to God. Both emphases are necessary for his argument. It is because he is Son of God that he has been set at God's right hand (1.5, 13), but it is because he is son of man that he has been crowned with glory and honour (2.6, 9): those whose humanity he shares are therefore delivered from death and share his glory (2.14f., 10). It is because he has been tested as we are that he is qualified to be a priest (4.14f.), but it is because he is a priest for ever, according to the order of Melchizedek (7.17), that he continues for ever and is always alive to make intercession for his people (7.25).

The sacrificial imagery employed by our author is used elsewhere in the New Testament (for example, in the idea of Christ as a Passover lamb),[14] but nowhere else is it explored as extensively as it is here. Hebrews is also unique in depicting Christ as high priest as well as victim (9.11f.) – though of course we do find in Paul the notion that Christ *gave himself* up to death:[15] the idea that Christ acted as high priest is another way of stressing the fact that he was not just a passive participant in events, but a willing one. It is because he is both priest and victim that the offering he makes is the perfect one – the complete response to God's

---

14　E.g. 1 Cor. 5.7; the Johannine passion narrative.
15　Gal. 2.20.

will (10.5–9) and by it *we* are sanctified (10.10) and so enabled to enter the sanctuary (10.19).

What does Christ's death achieve? Our author interprets it in terms of the imagery of the Day of Atonement: it is an atoning sacrifice which cleanses from sin. Christ is here identified with the goat whose blood was taken into the Holy of Holies by the high priest as a sacrifice 'for sins' (7.27; 9.7). Interestingly, our author does *not* identify him with the scapegoat – the second animal used in the ritual of the Day of Atonement, to whom the sins of Israel were 'transferred', and who was driven away into the wilderness. Jesus is holy and pure, his blood atones, he is *not* 'laden with sins'. And in offering the final sacrifice 'for sins' (10.12) he has entered the sanctuary (6.20) and come into the presence of God (9.24) 'on our behalf'. In these last two passages, we find the familiar phrase 'for us', used by our author in his own distinctive way, of Christ's ascension into heaven rather than of his death. In dying, he was identified with men and women – he 'tasted death for all' (2.9); in his resurrection/ ascension, they are identified with him, for he is their forerunner (6.20; cf. 2.10). Once again, we find echoes here of ideas that we have discovered already in Paul.

Like Paul, too, our author sees Christ's death and resurrection as a deliverance from death as well as from sin, but unlike Paul, he does not specifically relate these two ideas of sin and death. He tells us simply that Jesus shared our human flesh and blood, so that through his death he might destroy the one who has the power of death, namely the devil (2.14f.). The idea that the powers of evil are destroyed by Christ's death was perhaps a familiar one (certainly we have met it elsewhere), and our author is content here simply to state it, without offering any further explanation. But the idea that Christ identified himself with men and women is sufficient hint: he tastes death for all (2.9), but because his life could not be destroyed (7.16) the power of death itself is destroyed. Because his life could not be destroyed he entered heaven as our forerunner and representative (6.20, 9.24). As our high priest, he offered his own life in sacrifice, and his sacrifice has lasting validity because that self-offering was all that God required (10.5– 9); having made that complete sacrifice, he sat down at God's right hand. Because of the power of a life that cannot be destroyed we are able now to approach God (7.16–19). The basis of this conviction is, of course, the resurrection – as we are reminded in the description of God in 13.20 as the one who 'brought our Lord Jesus back from the dead'. Though the epistle seems to be dominated by the idea of Christ's death, therefore, his resurrection and exaltation – or, in priestly imagery, his entry into heaven – are just as significant. The efficacy of his self-offering is due to the fact that his life was not destroyed.

Christ shared human flesh and blood, and Christians, in turn, are called to identify with Christ – to go to him 'outside the camp', bearing his disgrace and prepared to share his suffering (13.12f.). Those who fall away from the faith, however, 'crucify the Son of God on their own account' (6.6) – that is, they align themselves with Jesus' enemies, and so share their guilt:[16] for them, says our author, there is no second chance to repent. Because Christ's death is a once-for-all event (9.26–8), it deals with sins once and for all at baptism – and one cannot crucify him again to obtain another new start. There is no further sacrifice to deal with the sins of those who, having once been cleansed from a guilty conscience, deliberately persist in sin (10.26f.). This rigorist teaching has greatly disturbed many later Christians, but we have to bear in mind that the author was thinking mainly of the sin of apostasy (as in 3.12). The problem became a very real one in times of persecution, when Christians faced with martyrdom lapsed from the faith and later repented.

Our author's conviction that Jesus' death was an expiatory sacrifice which dealt with the effects of sin has played an important part in subsequent understanding of the atonement. For many Christians, the belief that the blood of Jesus cleansed them from sin has been central to their faith. Yet today, many find the argument of the epistle strange and difficult to follow, for the simple reason that we live in a very different world, in which temple sacrifice is no longer part of our normal experience. We need to remember that our author was making use of ideas that were familiar to his audience – concepts that were part of the given structure of how things were – in order to try to show them the relevance of Christ's death to their lives. His analogies may not always be helpful to us – but we can at least appreciate his purpose in using them.

---

16 Since Jesus' death was 'once for all', it seems necessary to translate the verb *anastaurō* (used only here in the New Testament) by 'to crucify' (the meaning it always has in extra-biblical literature) rather than by 'to crucify again', as is commonly done. Cf. M. E. Isaacs, *Sacred Space*, Sheffield 1992, p. 93.

CHAPTER EIGHT

1 Peter – 1 John – Revelation

When we turn to the Catholic Epistles, we find that there is
no direct reference to the death and resurrection of Jesus in
James, 2 Peter, 2 and 3 John or Jude. There is so little
teaching in James that is specifically Christian that the
absence of a reference there is hardly surprising,[1] while the
other letters are so brief that the omission is insignificant:
even Paul could write at least one letter (Philemon[2]) without
mentioning the topic. The two letters which are important
for our theme are 1 Peter and 1 John, and in this chapter we
shall look at them, together with the book of Revelation. In
all three writings, we see authors interpreting Christ's death
and resurrection in ways relevant to the particular circumstances of their readers.

1 Peter

Those who maintain the traditional Petrine authorship of
this epistle naturally regard the letter as evidence for a very
early understanding of Christ's death. Those on the other
hand who believe that it was written in Peter's name after
his martyrdom see it as a somewhat later interpretation,
though one which made use of traditional material. Whatever we decide on this the letter is interesting, first of all
because it makes use both of ideas we have met elsewhere
and of interpretations which are new to us, and secondly
because of the way it applies teaching about Christ's death
to the problems confronting the letters' recipients.

---

1 One might, however, have expected even this author to appeal in 5.10f.
to Christ's steadfastness under suffering, rather than to the endurance of
the prophets and Job!
2 We may perhaps include 2 Thessalonians also, though many scholars
argue that this epistle was not written by Paul himself.

One of the prominent themes in this letter is the idea, already familiar to us from the rest of the New Testament, that the Christian community is the people of God. The author addresses his readers – as he might have addressed a group of Jews – as 'exiles of the dispersion' (1.1), who live in foreign lands. They have been chosen by God (1.2) – as were the original Israelites – to form ' a chosen race, a royal priesthood, a dedicated nation, a people for God's possession' (2.9).[3] It is not surprising, then, that in the wording of 1.2 – 'for obedience to Jesus Christ and sprinkling with his blood' – we are reminded of the covenant made between God and his people on Sinai, when they promised to obey his law, and Moses spattered them with blood as a sign that the covenant had been sealed (Ex. 24.7f.)[4]

Further references to this theme occur in 1.15f., in the command to be holy and the appeal to scripture (Lev. 11.44f.), which says 'You shall be holy because I am holy', and in the reminder that they were redeemed with the precious blood of Christ, like that of a lamb without defect or blemish (1.19). At this point the author might have in mind one of a variety of sacrificial lambs, and some commentators have also linked the imagery with that used in Isa. 53.7, but in view of the overall theme, and the use of the verb 'to redeem' (*lutroō*[5]), it seems most probable that this is a reference to the Passover lamb.[6] According to the story of Exodus 12, the blood of the original Passover lambs protected the Israelites from the destruction which annihilated all the firstborn Egyptians, and so led to the Exodus from Egypt: it was thus the means of the nation's redemption. But this new redemption in Christ's blood includes Gentiles, who were not members of Israel, since (echoing Hos. 2.23) the chosen race, who have been called out of darkness into light, consists of those who had been 'no people' but who are now the people of God, and those who had 'not received mercy' but who have now received mercy (2.9f.). This new act of redemption is no afterthought on God's part: Christ was predestined before the foundation of the world, though only recently revealed, so that through

---

3 Ex. 19.6; Isa. 43.20f.
4 The imagery of the new covenant, sealed by the sprinkling of Christ's blood (as it were, on the people), is found in Heb. 9.15–20.
5 The verb is used in the LXX of the Exodus (e.g. Ex.6.6; 13.13, 15) and of the hope of a future redemption, which is often depicted as a second Exodus (e.g. Isa. 35.9; 51.11; 52.3).
6 Cf. 1 Cor. 5.7; John 1.29; 2.13–22 (v. 13); 6.1–59 (v. 4); 18.28; 19.36.

him believers might trust in God who raised him from the dead and gave him glory (1.20f.).

This idea of the Christian community as the 'new' people of God, redeemed by Christ's death, is used by all the authors whose writings we have examined. Familiar, too, is this author's method of appealing to scripture, which backs up his comment in 1.10 that the salvation of which he writes was described by the prophets, who also predicted the sufferings and subsequent glory of Christ. Many of the passages he quotes are used by other New Testament writers – in particular, we recognize a familiar theme in the group of sayings about a stone in 2.6–8, used to support the idea that Christ is both a crucial corner-stone for believers,[7] and a cause of stumbling for unbelievers.[8]

One passage used by our author is Isaiah 53, but the quotations from that passage are introduced in a novel way. In 2.18ff. he addresses slaves who have the misfortune to belong to cruel masters, and encourages them by assuring them that when they suffer unjustly, they have the approval of God. He then explains that this is part of their calling, since Christ suffered for them, leaving them an example, that they should follow in his steps (2.21). The next few verses may well be an early 'hymn' – certainly the section begins, as other hymnic passages do, with an emphatic 'he'. Much of it echoes Isaiah 53: '. . . no deceit was found in his mouth (2.22) . . . He himself bore our sins . . . by his wounds you have been healed' (2.24). The whole passage clearly interprets Christ's death as dealing with sins – though how is not explained; we learn only that he suffered 'for' others,[9] that he was innocent, and that he 'bore our sins in his body on the tree'. This is not the language of sacrifice, since nothing tainted with sin could be offered on the altar; it suggests rather either the imagery of the scapegoat in Lev. 16.10–22, or the account of the treatment of the executed criminal in Deut. 21.23. Since the *body* of the latter was impaled on a *tree*,[10] we should perhaps see this second idea here – in

---

7 Quoting Isa. 28.16 and Ps. 118.22.

8 Isa. 8. 14f. The two texts from Isaiah are also combined in Rom. 9.33. Elsewhere we find *either* the idea of Christ as a corner-stone (Mark 12.10f.; Acts 4.11; Eph. 2.20) *or* the idea that he is an offence – a *skandalon* (the word used in 1 Pet. 2.8 to describe the stone) – that leads them to stumble (Mark 6.3; 14.27, 29; Rom. 11.9; 1 Cor. 1.23; Gal. 5.11).

9 The familiar phrase *huper humōn*, 'for you', is used.

10 The same Greek words, *sōma* and *xulon*, are used here and in the LXX of Deut. 21.23.

which case the idea is that sin is somehow removed, done away with, in the death and burial of the victim.[11] This is the first time that Isaiah 53 has been applied to Christ's death in the way that we expect – i.e., bringing out its salvific power. What is interesting is that it is introduced to back up the author's teaching about how slaves are to behave. Christ has given them an example (*hupogrammos*), since he too suffered though innocent, and they are to do what he did (2.21f.). Yet his death is clearly far more than an example, since it is through his wounds that we are healed: he carried our sins in order that we might have no part in sins, but live to righteousness (2.24). The thought here is very close to that which Paul expresses in Rom. 6.11, where Christ's death and resurrection mean that believers die to sin and live to righteousness.

Similar ideas occur again in the next chapter, this time addressed to the community in general. Those who suffer unjustly (3.14) may be comforted by the thought that Christ, too, suffered[12] 'once and for all, on account of our sins, the righteous for (*huper*) the unrighteous, in order that he might bring us to God' (3.18). Once again, our author appeals to Christ's death as an example, but quickly reminds us that it is far more than this: the idea that Christ's death gives us access to God is familiar to us from Hebrews, as well as from the Pauline literature.[13] This passage, also, sounds hymnic; it continues 'put to death in the flesh,[14] brought to life in the spirit'. These two phrases are reminiscent of other summaries of Christian faith – notably Rom. 1.3f. and 1 Tim. 3.16 – and remind us that the resurrection was understood, not as a mere resuscitation of flesh, but rather as a new mode of existence. Christ has now entered heaven and is at God's right hand, having angels, authorities and powers subject to him (3.22).

Applying this teaching to the lives of his readers, our author urges them to be prepared for suffering, knowing that Christ also endured suffering, and that those who suffer in the flesh have finished with sin and now pass their lives in accordance with the will of God (4.1f.).[15] They must

---

11 Cf. Gal. 3.13.
12 Some mss read 'suffered' (*epathen*), others 'died' (*apethanen*), but there is little difference in sense.
13 Rom. 5.2; Eph. 2.18; 3.12.
14 The word is *sarx*, 'flesh', not 'body', as in REB.
15 The exact meaning of v. 1 is very difficult to determine, but this summary conveys the general sense. Cf. the commentaries for a discussion of the problems.

therefore no longer live the life of pagans, as they did in the past (4.3f.). This section is reminiscent of Paul's teaching about the meaning of baptism in Romans 6, and it may be significant that baptism is also discussed in 1 Pet. 3.21. At any rate, at least three implications of Christ's death are to be found in these verses. First, there is the theme of imitation: Christians must be prepared to suffer unjustly, as did he. Secondly, his death is the means by which our sin is dealt with and by which we are brought to God. Thirdly, the 'dying to sin' must be worked out in the daily lives of believers.

In the course of this discussion in 3.13–4.6 we find an enigmatic reference to Christ preaching to the imprisoned spirits who had been disobedient in the past (3.19f.). Commentators disagree as to whether these 'spirits' refer to the spirits of the dead or to supernatural beings, though the reference to preaching to the dead in 4.6 supports the former interpretation. Whichever way we understand it, this passage introduces an idea we have not met elsewhere – though there are possible hints of it in the references to Christ's 'descent' into the abyss (Rom. 10.7 and Eph. 4.9) – namely, that in the interval between his death and resurrection, Christ preached to those in Hades.

Yet the basis of our salvation is not Christ's death alone but his resurrection, as we are reminded two verses later, in 3.21. This is, indeed, an important theme in the epistle. At the very beginning, we have a thanksgiving to God because in his great mercy he has caused us to be born again into a living hope by the resurrection of Jesus Christ from the dead (1.3). Later in that chapter, we are reminded that our trust is in God – who raised Christ from the dead and gave him glory (1.21). In 3.21f., the reference to the resurrection leads into the description of his exaltation. Similar themes are reflected in the assurance that God is glorified through Jesus Christ in 4.11, and two verses later, in the promise that when his glory is revealed, our joy will be unbounded.[16] In this last passage, our author reminds his readers yet again that those who suffer unjustly share in the sufferings of Christ (4.13), but this time he is thinking specifically of suffering 'as a Christian' (4.14, 16) – i.e., of persecution. It is those who share Christ's sufferings who will rejoice when his glory is revealed, because they will share in that glory also (4.13f.). The author himself writes as one who is both a

---

16 Cf. also 5.1, 4, 10.

witness to the sufferings of Christ and a participant in the glory to be revealed (5.1). Once again, in this notion that believers can expect to share both the suffering and the exaltation of Christ, we find ourselves on familiar ground.

1 John

The so-called first epistle of John is not really an 'epistle' at all – though it is not at all clear how we *should* describe it: certainly it is addressed to the needs of a particular community known to the author, and thus in a sense fulfils the purpose of an epistle. There is considerable debate regarding authorship: some believe that it was written by the author of the Fourth Gospel, others that it was composed by someone else, living in the same community, who was addressing a somewhat changed situation. There are both similarities and differences in ideas in the two writings, and these could be explained on either hypothesis.

In the opening chapter the author reminds his readers that they live in light, not in darkness, and that this means that they are in fellowship with one another, and that the blood – that is the death – of Jesus cleanses them from all sin (1.7). In order to understand precisely what he means here we have to look at the structure of the whole paragraph, which unfortunately is slightly disguised by the way the chapters have been divided. When we do this, we see that 1.5–2.2 consists of an initial statement, 'God is light, and in him there is no darkness at all', followed by a series of six 'if' clauses arranged in three contrasting pairs. The first clause of each pair introduces a false claim, the second the proper course of action:

1 '*If we say* that we are in fellowship with him and go on living in darkness,
     we lie and not do what is true.
2 *But if* we live in light, as he is in the light,
     then we are in fellowship with one another and the blood of Jesus cleanses us from all sin.
3 *If we say* that we have no sin,
     we deceive ourselves and the truth is not in us.
4 *If* we confess our sin,
     he who is faithful and righteous will forgive us our sins and cleanse us from all unrighteousness.

5 *If we say* that we have not sinned,
   we make him a liar, and his word is not in us . . . .
6 *If* anyone sins,
   we have an advocate with the Father, Jesus Christ the
   righteous. He is the atoning sacrifice for our sins – not
   ours only, but those of the whole world.'

The rejection of three false claims suggests that the author
has in mind someone who is making them, and since in the
rest of the epistle we find indications of a serious split that
has recently taken place in the community and that has led
to a group of dissidents leaving (2.18f.), it may well be these
people whom he is attacking here. They are apparently
claiming to be without sin, and this leads our author to
stress the reality of sin and the power of Christ's death to
deal with sins.

In 1.7 he speaks of the blood of Jesus cleansing us from
sin, language that echoes that used of the Old Testament sin-
offerings (including those offered on the Day of Atonement)
which cleansed the worshippers from sin (Lev. 16.30),
language which we have already met in Hebrews (e.g. 9.22).
In 1 John 2.2 our author describes Christ as an 'atoning
sacrifice' – the Greek word is *hilasmos*, which is used only
twice in the New Testament, the other occurrence being at
4.10.[17] In the LXX, we find this word used of the sin-
offering, whose purpose was to remove sin (Lev. 25.9). In
the account of what happened on the Day of Atonement in
Lev. 16.16, we find the cognate verb (*exilaskesthai*) used,
and its meaning is clearly 'to cleanse' or 'purify'. Since the
Hebrew verb used here is *kipper*, and since the Greek verb
meaning 'to cleanse' (*katharizō*) used in 1 John 1.7 and 9 is
also frequently used to translate *kipper*, it seems probable

---

17 The word is related to *hilasterion*, a means of expiation, used in Rom.
3.25 (see above, pp. 41f.) and Heb. 9.5, and also to the verb *hilaskesthai*,
to make expiation, passive, be merciful, used in Luke 18.13; Heb. 2.17.
Both words are common in the LXX. There has been a great deal of
discussion as to how *hilasmos* should be translated. 'Propitiation',
'expiation' and 'atonement' have all been suggested. Outside the biblical
literature, the word and its cognates are often used in the sense of
propitiating the gods, but in the Old Testament God is not the object of
what is done. The purpose of the *hilasmos* is rather to deal with the sin
that has come between God and his people, so that the verb *hilaskesthai*
has the sense of 'forgive' or 'cleanse'. 'Expiation' is thus a better word
than 'propitiation', but we have followed the NRSV (and REB) in spelling
this out as 'atoning sacrifice', in order to bring out the link with the
ceremony of the Day of Atonement.

that our author had in mind throughout this section the ceremony of the Day of Atonement.[18] When we discover that the word *hilasmos* can also mean 'forgiveness' (as in Ps. 130.4), one of the ideas expressed in 1.9, we realize how closely parallel these three verses are.

And indeed, when we look more closely at the six lines, we realize that there is a close similarity between lines 1, 3 and 5, as well as between 2, 4 and 6, which can be seen more easily if we spell out the second part of each line:

1 we *lie* and do not do what is true (*lit.*: do not do *the truth*)
3 we deceive ourselves and *the truth is not in us*
5 we make him a *liar*, and his word is *not in us*

'Lie' and 'deceit' are synonyms; so are 'the truth' and 'God's word': the three statements are thus closely parallel.

2 the blood of Jesus *cleanses us* from all *sin*
4 he who is faithful and *righteous* will forgive us our *sins and cleanse us* from all unrighteousness
6 Jesus Christ the *righteous* is the atoning sacrifice for our *sins* – not ours only, but those of the whole world

We have already seen that there is a close link between cleansing, forgiving, and the atoning sacrifice.

So why does our author make his point three times? Is this mere rhetoric? Does he think it necessary to hammer the point home? Or is the significance of the repetitions to be found in the variations? It seems very likely that he is attacking the beliefs of those who have left his community, and that this group believed themselves to have obtained perfection, and were therefore refusing to acknowledge the possibility that they could sin. Though they claimed to be in fellowship with God, they were in fact living in darkness (1.6), and were totally insensitive to the difference between right and wrong, refusing to admit that they were guilty of sin (1.8) or that they had committed sin (1.10). In making these claims, these people presumably meant that they had not committed sin *since becoming Christians*. Like some of Paul's converts, they were interpreting too literally the teaching that sin had no place in the Christian life: instead of acknowledging their failures they denied them. Our author recognizes that sin is all too possible for Christians: certainly they *ought* to live in the light, and he writes to urge his community *not* to sin – but if anyone *does* sin, then there is

18 Cf. once again Rom. 3.25 and Hebrews 9.

a remedy available in the person of Jesus Christ: he is an advocate on their behalf with the Father, and his death is an atoning sacrifice still for their sins, and for those of the whole world. This passage sounds a much more positive note regarding post-baptismal sin than do Heb. 6.4–6 and 10.26, which insisted on the 'pastness' of Christ's death, but we have to remember that those passages were about former Christians who committed apostasy: 1 John is equally harsh about those who denied what he believed to be the heart of the Christian faith, whom he describes in 2.18 as 'anti-christs'.

After this emphatic teaching, we may well feel puzzled when we come to chapter 3 and find our author himself arguing that those who dwell in Christ do not sin, and that those who *do* sin are children of the devil, not of God (3.4–9; cf. 5.18)! It seems that he wishes to eat his cake and have it. Yet the problem he is struggling with is common enough, and we ought to recognize it. Christians *have* been removed from darkness to light; their sins *have* been forgiven; they *do* know God; they *have* overcome the evil one (2.11–13). If they dwell in Christ, in whom there is no sin, then they *should* not sin (3.5f.). This is the ideal he sets before his readers. Yet he knows that Christians are fallible, and it is noticeable that he does not use the first person in describing this state of sinlessness. The trouble with those whose views he attacks is that they apparently *do* claim to be 'without sin'. Like John Wesley, our author has a doctrine of Christian perfection, but is suspicious of those who claim to *be* perfect! Behind his apparently contradictory statements we recognize the truth that the Christian is, in Luther's phrase, *simul justus et peccator* – at one and the same time justified and yet a sinner.

There are three further references to the death of Christ in 1 John. The first is in 3.16: 'this is how we know love: he laid down his life for us'. Once again we have the familiar phrase 'for us', but there is no explanation here as to what this 'for us' might mean. The sentence occurs in a section urging Christians to love one another, so that it is not surprising that Christ's action is seen as an *example* to be followed: 'and we ought to lay down our lives for fellow-Christians.'

The second reference (in 4.10) is also found in a section that is concerned with the theme of love, and follows a statement that is closely parallel to John 3.16f.: 'God sent his only Son into the world in order that we might live

through him. In this is love – not that we loved God but that
he loved us – and sent his son as an atoning sacrifice
(*hilasmos*) for our sins'. This spells out, as John 3.16f. does
not, the way in which God saves the world through Christ,
but adds nothing to what we have already been told about
his death in 2.2. Once again, as in 3.16, the 'moral' drawn is
that Christians should love each other in the same way.

The final reference is in 5.6–8, in the enigmatic statement
that Christ came 'by water and by blood'. Whatever may be
the significance of these words, the term 'blood' presumably
refers to Christ's death, and the passage thus affirms the
importance of that event for Christian belief.

Revelation

The book we know as 'The Revelation of John' or 'The
Apocalypse' is perhaps the most difficult one in the whole
New Testament for us to understand today. The title means
'uncovering' or 'disclosure', and the book purports to reveal
the secrets of history and what is going to take place. Like all
apocalyptic writing, it uses symbolism which would probably have been clear at the time but whose meaning is now
hidden from us, though part of it can be comprehended from
some of the many Old Testament passages to which the
author alludes. John[19] uses this genre of writing in order to
convey to his readers his message of final victory for Christ
and for those who are faithful to him. The situation of the
various communities whom he addresses was not necessarily
the same – what he says to the seven churches in chapters 2–
3 suggests that they may have had very different problems
and temptations – but his message is nevertheless relevant to
them all.[20] The book reflects an experience of persecution,
but this is not necessarily taking place at the time that he
writes – indeed, it would seem from his remarks to some of
the seven churches that their problem was rather that of
complacency and of compromise with Rome than persecu-

---

19 Tradition assumed that the 'John' of 1.1 was also the author of the
Fourth Gospel and the Johannine Epistles, but the style, language and
ideas of this book are so different from the other four that as long ago as
the third century Dionysius, bishop of Alexandria, recognized that the
John who wrote Revelation could not have been the author of the Gospel
or the Epistles.

20 Richard Bauckham, *The Theology of the Book of Revelation*, CUP
1993, pp. 12–17, has an interesting discussion of this.

tion.[21] His message would have brought comfort and encouragement to some, warning and challenge to others.

John presents Jesus as the one who through death has become king, who has conquered already and will conquer again: those who share his sufferings are promised a share in his triumph. This theme is introduced in the opening greeting and doxology in 1.5f., where Jesus is described as the 'faithful witness'. Because those who witnessed to their Christian faith in the early days often suffered death, the word *martus* which is used here came to have the sense of 'martyr'; it is used in 2.13 and 17.6 of those who died for their faith. So the reference to Jesus here and in 3.14 as a 'faithful witness'[22] reminds us already of his death. The next phrase tells us that he is 'the firstborn from the dead' – a phrase used also in Col. 1.18.[23] He is also Lord – 'the ruler of the kings of the earth' – the result, as we already know, of his resurrection and exaltation.[24]

This summary leads into the ascription of glory 'to him who loves us and has set us free[25] from our sins with his blood'. The image is again that of the Exodus and the Passover lamb, by whose blood the Israelites were set free from Egypt;[26] this new redemption, however, is 'from our sins'.[27] Exodus language is continued in the statement that he has made us 'a kingdom, priests to his God and Father'. This somewhat cryptic summary echoes the promise of Ex. 19.6, which is also taken up in 1 Pet. 2.9. The idea that Christ's death and resurrection are a great victory which rescues men and women from sin and death and creates an eschatological community sets the tone for the whole book. In the vision of Christ at the end of chapter 1, for example, he is said to be the living one who was dead and who is alive for evermore, and to hold the keys of death and Hades (1.18): it is because of his own death and resurrection that Christ now exercises divine control over the power of death and can set men and women free from Hades.

Similarly, it is because of his death that he is able to redeem men and women, and having himself received

---

21 John Sweet, *Revelation*, SCM Pelican Commentary 1979, pp. 26f.
22 The same phrase is used in 2.13 of the martyr Antipas.
23 For a similar idea, see 1 Cor. 15.20.
24 1 Cor. 15.24–8; Phil. 2.9–11.
25 The variant reading 'washed' (*lousanti*) is found in some mss, but 'set us free' (*lusanti*) has better support and fits the context better.
26 See above, note 6, and 1 Pet. 1.18f.
27 Cf. 1 Cor. 15.3.

honour and glory he is able to share his rule with those
whom he brings into God's kingdom (5.6–14). The vision of
the Lamb, 'standing as though slain' – in other words, with
the marks of sacrifice plainly visible (5.6) – picks up the
theme of 1.5f. There is nothing to indicate which particular
Old Testament sacrifice the author had in mind, and (as in
John 1.29) the image may be open-ended. Some commentators suggest that Isa. 53.7 has influenced the author of
Revelation here; certainly the Passover lamb is again
relevant.[28] The Lamb is greeted by the four living creatures
round God's throne and by the twenty-four elders as the one
who is worthy to open the scroll which will reveal the secret
purpose of God – in particular, the way in which those who
share Christ's witness, sacrifice and victory will participate
in God's kingdom. He is worthy to do this because he was
slain and by his blood has redeemed people for God from
every tribe and language, nation and race. He has made
them a kingdom and priests for our God, and they will reign
on the earth (5.9–10). Once again, we have the familiar
Exodus imagery: Christ has redeemed (or ransomed)[29] his
people, and established a kingdom of priests (Ex. 19.6).
Then the whole company of heaven joins in a paean of
praise to the Lamb who was slain, and who is worthy 'to
receive power and wealth and wisdom and might and
honour and glory and blessing' (5.12): because of his
sacrifice, he receives the honours due to God himself.

The Lamb is a central figure in Revelation, reminding us
of the importance of Christ's sacrificial death and resurrection. His blood will make white the robes of those who
endure the final tribulation (7.14), but he will bring wrath
upon the wicked (6.16). It is by the blood of the Lamb, and
by their own witness – in word and by their deaths – that
the martyrs share his defeat of Satan (12.11); the names of
his followers are written in the book of the Lamb, who was
slain from the foundation of the world.[30] The Lamb stands
on Mount Zion in triumph, with the one hundred and forty-
four thousand who have been ransomed (*agorazō*) from the
earth as the firstfruits of the human race for God and the
Lamb (14.1–5). He will defeat the satanic powers that attack

---

28 The word for 'lamb', *arnion*, is rare in the LXX; it is, however, used in
Jer. 11.19, which could have influenced the imagery here.
29 The verb is *agorazō* lit. 'to buy': cf. 1 Cor. 6.20; 7.23; also *exagorazō*
Gal. 3.13; 4.5.
30 NRSV takes this last phrase with 'written' on the analogy of 17.8, but
the order of the Greek is against this.

him (17.14). At the end of the book the company of heaven celebrate the marriage of the Lamb (19.7, 9). In the new Jerusalem there is no need of temple or of light, because God and the Lamb are both its temple and its light.

Those who follow the Lamb can expect to share his suffering, and there are frequent references to 'the blood of God's people'.[31] But they will share also in his victory. In 15.3 they sing the song of Moses and the song of the Lamb — a reminder that the victory of the Lamb is a redemption comparable to the Exodus.[32] The death and resurrection of Jesus ensure the final defeat of Satan and the victory of truth over the lie, for he is the one who is 'Faithful and True', and his name is 'the Word of God' (19.11–13), whereas the beast is the source of lies and delusions (v. 20). Jesus' followers are those who keep God's commandments and maintain their witness to Jesus (12.17), who is himself the faithful and true witness (3.14) and the Amen, the very embodiment of truth.[33]

Throughout this book, then, the death of Christ is seen as a great redemptive act which brings God's people into being, and which ensures the final victory over the forces of evil.

* * *

We have looked in this chapter at three very different books, written by different authors and addressing different circumstances. The death of Christ is of central importance in each of them, though as we might expect, each author handles it in a different way. 1 Peter and Revelation have many themes in common: both are heavily dependent on Old Testament imagery and interpret Jesus' death as a Passover sacrifice, his death and resurrection as a second Exodus which creates a new people of God; both expect Christians, as members of that new community, to share in the sufferings of Christ and in his final vindication. 1 John makes less use of Old Testament imagery, though the idea of the community as the people of God whose sins are dealt with by the atoning death of Jesus is fundamental. Like 1 Peter, 1 John uses the traditional formula 'for us', and all three writers see the death of Jesus as an example to be followed — or rather, to be shared. 1 John speaks of Christians having overcome the

---

31 16.6; 17.6; 18.24; 19.2. Cf. 6.10.
32 This section is full of Exodus imagery — the sea in 15.2, the song in vv. 3f., the plagues in 16, and a reminiscence of the theophany on Sinai in 16.18.
33 *Amen* means 'true'.

evil one, while Revelation spells out the future defeat of the satanic forces. But as well as what they have in common each writer, as we have seen, has his own distinctive contribution to make. Different images are appropriate in different situations, but fundamental to all these authors is the belief that the death and resurrection of Christ are the great redemptive act by which God has brought a new community into being.

Epilogue

As we have seen, our New Testament writers employ a great variety of images in attempting to explain the significance of Jesus' death. There is no one 'orthodox' view, since all attempts to explain the inexplicable must inevitably be inadequate. Faced with a mystery which could not be grasped, these men could only search for metaphors in hope of expressing something of their experience of reconciliation with God.

Yet however diverse their interpretations, they have an underlying unity. All of them begin from the conviction that what had happened was the work of God. Even though Jesus was put to death through the weakness and sin of wicked men and the rebellion of satanic powers, it was part of God's plan, and took place in accordance with scripture.

Our writers are agreed, too, that the death and resurrection of Jesus must be seen together: his death is meaningless until God gives it significance by raising him to life. Even when the resurrection is not specifically mentioned, it is assumed: the verdict pronounced upon Jesus has been overthrown, and he has been vindicated, exalted, given authority. The victory is essential, and it is only in the light of the resurrection that Jesus' death can be reinterpreted.

Basic to all our authors, too, is the conviction that through Christ's death and resurrection God has reconciled us to himself. The language is Paul's (2 Cor 5.18f.), but the idea is common to all. Men and women are made members of God's people – the new 'Israel'; Jews and Gentiles alike become children of God. These ideas are based on the tradition of the special relationship between God and Israel, and the language used to describe the new development is naturally taken from the Old Testament. Christians have been redeemed, Christ's death replaces the Passover, and a new Exodus and a new covenant establish a new community – the community of those who (in Pauline terms) are 'in

Christ', and who share his death and resurrection. Nor is the notion that disciples must share Christ's death and resurrection merely metaphorical: for many of our writers, the possibility of sharing Christ's sufferings is all too real. Paul certainly knows what it is to suffer hardship and persecution. Mark – and Matthew also – seems to have been very conscious of the cost of discipleship. Luke sees 'bearing the cross' as a daily challenge. The authors of both Hebrews and 1 Peter allude to persecution, and the persecution of the saints, who share the sufferings and the victory of the Lamb, is a central theme in Revelation. The idea that Jesus suffered 'for us' does not mean that Christians can expect to escape suffering themselves – the very opposite! Christ triumphs over death, but those who want to share his triumph must share his shame and suffering and death.

All our writers, then, are very much aware of the 'shame' of the gospel – of the scandal of the cross. It is not simply the absurdity of the gospel itself – a crucified Messiah! – which might cause Christians to blush, but its implications for the life-style of those who commit themselves to following a crucified Lord. Men and women of the ancient world, as of the late twentieth century, set great store by honour and prestige, wealth and possessions. John and James thought that following Jesus entitled them to a share in his glory and authority (Mark 10.35–7); the Corinthians assumed that the gospel would make them rich and powerful (1 Cor. 4.8). Jesus had to remind his disciples that following him meant drinking his cup and sharing his baptism, without looking for reward or honour (Mark 10.38–40). Paul insists that response to the gospel means accepting shame and weakness, poverty and want, persecution and slander (1 Cor. 4.9–13); but he has gladly given up every human privilege for the sake of gaining Christ, and so of sharing his sufferings and his resurrection.

It is clear that many of those who heard the gospel shied away from it. Even some of those who accepted it were somewhat embarrassed by it, and succumbed to the temptation to 'forget' the cross and its implications: a gospel of power and glory was so much more acceptable than one of weakness and shame! Our New Testament writers are united in insisting that the cross is the heart of the gospel: if the death of Christ is meaningless without the resurrection, so, too, the resurrection depends for its significance on the crucifixion. In seeking to explain *how* Christ could have been crucified, they uncovered deep veins of meaning in all that had taken place. They did not shy away from the cross but embraced it – and in doing so, discovered that weakness was turned to strength, foolishness became wisdom, and shame was revealed as true glory (1 Cor. 1.18–31). By the time our fourth evangelist came to write, he was so insistent on this theme that it quite transformed the story: glory and shame had coalesced, so that Jesus was 'exalted' on the cross and 'glorified' by his death. In the ancient world, the absurdity of this idea would have been so apparent that no-one would have missed the paradox in his presentation: centuries later, readers might easily misunderstand John's purpose and forget the reality of the shame and suffering which are transformed by the power of the resurrection.[1]

The idea – common to Paul and John – that God's glory is revealed in the death of Christ is perhaps the New Testament's most profound insight into its meaning. For the background of the Greek word for glory (*doxa*) is the Hebrew *kābōd* – a word which is used to express what God is. The belief that God is revealed in the shame and weakness of the cross is a profound insight into the nature of God. 'Anyone who has seen me has seen the Father,' says the Johannine Jesus to his disciples (John 14.9). In the cross, claims Paul, the *power* of God is revealed (1 Cor. 1.18). By embracing the scandal of the cross, and joyfully accepting its shame, these early Christians discovered the true character of God, and found that the true source of joy consisted in becoming like him.

---

1 The paradox is well-expressed in the first line of John Bowring's hymn, 'In the Cross of Christ I glory'.

Select Bibliography

Caird, G. B., *Principalities and Powers*, OUP 1956
Grayston, K., *Dying, We Live*, Darton Longman and Todd 1990
Hengel, M., *Crucifixion*, SCM 1977
Hengel, M., *The Atonement*, SCM 1981
Knox, J., *The Death of Christ*, Collins 1959
Martin, R. P., *Reconciliation: A Study of Paul's Theology*,
 Marshall Morgan and Scott 1981
Moule, C. F. D., *The Sacrifice of Christ*, Hodder and Stoughton
 1956
Stanley, D. M., *Christ's Resurrection in Pauline Soteriology*,
 Analecta Biblica 1961
Tannehell, R. C., *Dying and Rising with Christ*, Töpelmann 1967
Weber, H.-R., *The Cross*, SPCK 1979
Young, F. M., *Sacrifice and the Death of Christ*, SPCK 1975
Young, F. M., *Can These Dry Bones Live?* SCM 1982

Index of Modern Authors